PERENNIALS

The American Horticultural Society
Illustrated Encyclopedia of Gardening

PERENNIALS

The American Horticultural Society
Mount Vernon, Virginia

For the American Horticultural Society

President
Dr. Gilbert S. Daniels

Technical Advisory Committee
Everett Conklin
Mary Stuart Maury
Dr. John A. Wott

Perennials Staff for The Franklin Library/Ortho Books

Editorial Director
Min S. Yee

Supervisory Editor
Lewis P. Lewis

Editor
Ken Burke

Art Directors
John Williams
Barbara Ziller

Creative Director
Michael Mendelsohn

Assistant Creative Director
Clint Anglin

Contributing Writers
A. Cort Sinnes
Michael D. McKinley

Manuscript Consultants
Pamela J. Harper
Seaford, Virginia

George H. Scott
Arcadia, California

Carl A. Totemeier
Old Westbury Gardens
Old Westbury, New York

Illustrator
Cyndie Clark-Huegel

Production Director
Robert Laffler

Production Manager
Renee Guilmette

For Ortho Books

Publisher
Robert L. Iacopi

For The Franklin Library

Publisher
Joseph Sloves

The pink peonies *(Paeonia)* on the front cover are just one of the many favorite perennials for today's garden. Their large, fragrant flowers come in many forms and colors, and the plants are extremely long-lived. Photograph by Derek Fell.

Contributing Photographers
(Names of photographers in alphabetical order are followed by page numbers on which their work appears. R = right, C = center, L = left, T = top, B = bottom

William C. Aplin
16T, 68B, 123C

John Blaustein
43, 44, 48, 141

Josephine Coatsworth
17, 20, 23CL,BL, 30T,B, 31, 33, 40, 45, 47, 51, 56, 60T, 61, 65, 66, 76B, 82R, 83TL,TR, 84, 95

Derek Fell
22T, 78, 88, 89T, 91, 93 96, 99, 101TR, 102TL, 103B, 106, 109T, 122, 124, 125, 126, 128C, 132T, 137T, 139B

Pamela Harper
13, 14–15, 18T, 19, 23TL, TR, CR, 24, 53, 68T, 69B, 70, 77T, 79T,R, 81, 92, 98, 100, 101B, 102TR, 112, 114, 115T,B, 116B, 121T, 123B, 128B, 129T,B, 130B, 136, 139T

Dmitri Kessel, Life Magazine © 1980 Time Inc.
62T

Michael Landis
80C, 82L, 94C

Michael McKinley
8, 10, 11, 16B, 18L, 21, 23BR, 32, 34, 36, 38, 41, 58B, 67, 73T,B, 74, 76T, 77B, 80B, 85, 86, 87, 94T,B, 101TL, 102B, 103TR, 104, 105T,B, 107R (T-B), 109B, 110, 111, 113, 116T, 117T, 119T,B, 121B, 123T, 128T, 130C, 131, 132B, 133T,B, 134, 135T,RT, 137B, 138

James K. McNair
22B, 71B, 118

Musee Marmattan, Institut de France, Paris
62L

National Portrait Gallery, London, England
58T, 60B

Ortho Photo Collection
37, 63, 83B, 107T, 108, 120 130T, 140

George Taloumis
52, 69R, 71T, 72, 75, 89B, 90, 97, 117B, 127T,B, 135BR

Tom Tracy
103TL

Photo Stylist
Sara Slavin
43, 44, 48, 141

Photo Sources
Arthur Hecht
San Rafael, California

The Bailey Arboretum
Oyster Bay, New York

Bluebird Nursery
Nebraska

Boerner Gardens of Whitnall Park
Hales Corner, Wisconsin

Cantigny Estate
Wheaton, Illinois

The Case Estates of Arnold Arboretum
Weston, Massachusetts

Charles Wilson
of Joseph Harris Co., Inc.
Rochester, New York

The Chicago Botanic Garden
Chicago, Illinois

The Denver Botanic Garden
Denver, Colorado

Dick Turner,
San Francisco, California

Dodge Freeman, Designer,
Lake Forest, Illinois

Frank Cabot
Province of Quebec
Canada

Fred McGourty,
Brooklyn Botanic Garden,
Brooklyn, New York

Harold Epstein
Larchmont, New York

Jack Romine,
Walnut Creek, California

Jane Gates,
of the Helen Crocker Russell Memorial Library
of Strybing Arboreteum Society
Golden Gate Park, San Francisco, California

John Bryan
San Rafael, California

Sir John R. H. Thuron
Unionville, Pennsylvania

Judy Glattstein, Designer
Oyster Bay, New York

Longwood Gardens,
Kennett Square, Pennsylvania

Marilyn Alimo, President,
The Garden Clubs of Illinois

Oehme, Van Sweden and Associates, Inc.
Washington, D.C.

Old Westbury Gardens
Old Westbury, New York

Paul Sibbitt
Novato, California

Peggy Keener
San Anselmo, California

Spring Hill Gardens
Mentor, Ohio

Wave Hill
Bronx, New York

Western Hills Nursery
Occidental, California

White Flower Farm
Litchfield, Connecticut

Produced under the authorization of The American Horticultural Society by The Franklin Library and Ortho Books.

Copyright © 1981 by Ortho Books. Special contents © 1982 by The American Horticultural Society. All rights reserved under International and Pan-American Copyright Conventions.

Every effort has been made at the time of publication to guarantee the accuracy of the names and addresses of information sources and suppliers and in the technical data contained. However, the subscriber should check for his own assurance and must be responsible for selection and use of suppliers and supplies, plant materials, and chemical products.

No portion of this book may be reproduced in any form or by any means without permission first being requested and obtained in writing from The American Horticultural Society, c/o The Franklin Library, Franklin Center, Pennsylvania, 19091. Portions of this volume previously appeared in the Ortho Book *All About Perennials*.

Library of Congress Catalog Card Number 81-71124

Printed in the United States of America

12 11 10 9 8 7 6 5 4 3 2

A Special Message from
The American Horticultural Society

The yearly rebirth of perennials and their constant, ever-changing succession of flowers and foliage through the seasons make them a lasting pleasure of gardening life. Perennials give a satisfaction over the years that far outlives the undeniable but ephemeral beauty of annuals.

There are perennials for every type of garden—big gardens or small, shady or sunny, moist or dry. There are tall perennials, short ones, and ones in between. Among them are ornamental grasses, foliage plants, a profusion of flowering plants, and even ornamental vegetables that can make stunning accents in the garden. The possible combinations are legion, from the traditional cottage garden, to modern "color masses," to gardens based on a single color scheme. Decades ago, Vita Sackville-West, the English novelist and horticulturist, developed a "tonal" garden of gray, green, and white at her home at Sissinghurst Castle that continues to intrigue gardeners all over the world. This unusual and striking garden may not be to everyone's liking, but it is an example of how the principle of tonal experimentation can be adapted by anyone, anywhere.

Combinations of color and texture are important in any garden, but a certain amount of planning and thought must go into the laying out of a perennial garden. Although changes can be made, and should be made if the initial result is not satisfactory, one of the chief joys of perennials is their permanence. True, some need tending in the way of dividing or other forms of occasional rejuvenation, but most require a minimum of maintenance and last for generations, once established.

Perennials can be successfully and artfully planted along with annuals, bulbs, and shrubs, and this is a common, even preferred practice with many gardeners. For example, perennials provide a permanent framework for the longer-lasting, more vibrant colors of annuals. And the combinations available in a mixed garden are far more varied than in a garden made up exclusively of either perennials or annuals.

Perennials is a valuable addition to our *Illustrated Encyclopedia of Gardening*. This book will add diversity and a new dimension to your gardening knowledge by helping you make the most of what gardeners all over the world consider their traditional and favorite garden flowers.

Gilbert S. Daniels

Gilbert S. Daniels
President

CONTENTS

The nature, virtues, and advantages of perennials have made them prominent favorites in gardens for generations. The world of perennials is a vast one, offering not only a great variety of attractive colors and textures but also a permanence that saves time, labor, and money every year. With perennials in your garden, you share in a rich heritage of beauty.

Thoughtful planning is important before planting perennials in a garden. These versatile plants lend themselves to many types of designs. Examples of the styles of gardens that have developed over the years will be found here, along with suggestions for creative plans, both traditional and modern, for planting and display.

THE TRADITIONAL FLOWERS

*Perennials are year-in, year-out
favorites. They can provide a lifetime
of pleasure with a minimum of care.*

To many people perennials seem like old-fashioned flowers. They conjure up memories of grandmother's garden or pictures of those beautiful borders that the English create so well. And, in fact, perennials are old-fashioned. They have been the favorites of generations of gardeners. But they are also the favorites of many gardeners today, and for the same reasons as in the past: they are relatively easy to grow, last from year to year, and offer an abundance of flowers in a great variety of colors and forms.

What distinguishes perennials from other plants? The best way to understand the difference is to compare them with annuals and biennials.

Annuals are plants that complete their entire life cycle in a year or less. In most cases, annuals are planted from seed in the spring, flower and set seed during the summer and early fall, and are killed by the first hard frosts of winter.

Biennials take 2 years to complete their life cycle. When grown from seed, the first year they produce leafy growth but usually no flowers; the second year they produce flowers, set seed, and die.

Perennials are plants that live more than 2 years. Many plants are perennial, including trees, shrubs, and some bulbs; but the word as used commonly and in this book refers to perennial flowering plants that are *herbaceous*, meaning that their stems are soft and fleshy rather than woody as with shrubs and trees. (Bulbs are classified separately because of their method of storing food.)

Woody shrubs and trees survive winters because their stems and trunks resist extreme cold. Herbaceous perennials survive varying degrees of winter cold because their roots are stronger and more vigorous than those of annuals and biennials. With the onset of cold, the tops of perennials die down, but the roots remain alive in a dormant state, sending forth new foliage and flowers each year when the weather warms. If growing conditions are right, this pattern can continue for many years—some perennials, for example peonies, gas plant, bleeding heart, and hosta, have been known to outlive their owners.

The long life of perennials gives the gardener some outstanding benefits. Their continual reappearance in the garden saves the time, labor, and expense of replanting every year. In addition, they provide a kind of permanent framework around which temporary plants can be placed. This gives a valuable continuity and coherence to the garden from one year to the next.

There are other advantages to perennials as well. Plants well adapted to your climate and planted in the right location will require very little attention. And since most perennials spread by underground buds that generate new plants, they can supply you with vigorous new stock ready for transplanting.

The simple lines of a formal garden offer an ideal setting for displaying masses of perennial blossoms. This is one of the classic gardens at Old Westbury Gardens in New York.

Most intriguing for many gardeners is that perennials come in an astonishing profusion of form, color, shape, and size, and there are literally thousands of varieties available. This incredible diversity makes even the mere planning of a perennial garden an exciting and rewarding experience.

Ideas and Information about Perennials

This book is both an idea book and a book of basic information. It contains ideas for combining and using perennials in many ways, and it also gives you the practical information you need to create your own beautiful perennial garden.

If you are interested in planning a garden but don't know how and where to begin, read *Planning a Perennial Garden*, beginning on page 12. This section will tell you everything you need to know to plan the garden, from how to use perennials as spot plantings to actually laying out a plan for formal or informal beds or borders. You'll find valuable advice on choosing colors and how to mix them, and all the details you need to know to select your plants. There are some solid guidelines on the trickiest aspect of perennial gardening—how to coordinate bloom cycles to achieve the effects you want. You'll also find information on the mixed perennial border and on an exciting new way to use perennials. In addition, you can learn about the cutting garden and perennials in containers.

For the information you need to grow the healthiest and most beautiful perennials, see *Basic Care and Culture*, page 42. This section will tell you how to get your soil into excellent condition, where to find the best plants, and how to start your own from seed. You'll also find information on fertilizing, watering, mulching, and on pest and disease control.

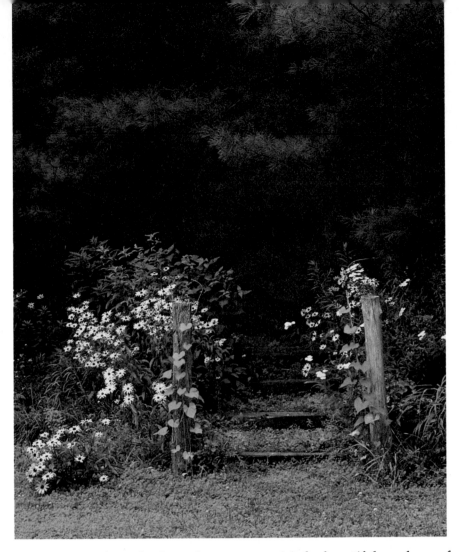

Even a few perennials scattered about the landscape can have great effect. Here an informal planting of yellow rudbeckias provides a welcome invitation to explore the rest of the garden.

For a leisurely tour through some exquisitely beautiful gardens of the past, see *The Art of Perennial Gardening*, starting on page 56. Some of these gardens, created by unusually gifted and famous gardeners, have profoundly influenced perennial gardening throughout the world, and continue to do so today. They may serve as the inspiration you need.

And finally, the *Plant Selection Guide*, starting on page 64, is an invaluable reference for gardeners just beginning with perennials and for veterans as well. The guide lists more than one hundred different perennials commonly grown in the United States. To help you visualize your projected garden and learn to identify the plants, there are photographs of every entry. You'll also find the hard facts of culture, and more detailed information on problem areas and on special ways to get the best health and bloom from each plant.

Plan Ahead

When you set out to create a beautiful garden there are many practical matters to be considered, especially in the vast world of perennials—the design of the garden, plant sources, all the cultural requirements, and much more.

Gardeners can be among the most inspired and talented people when it comes to the task of creating a beautiful environment. Transforming bare ground into a garden filled with colors, fragrance, the play of light and shadow, and sounds of birds and falling water can be almost magical.

In many cases the photographs in this book have caught that magic. By no means should you, as the reader, feel any hesitation if you want to recreate, perhaps identically, some of the scenes presented on the following pages. They are meant as an inspiration, the inspiration for anyone to create the special magic of a garden.

PLANNING A PERENNIAL GARDEN

A bed or border of perennials can be planned for sequence of bloom throughout the seasons, for contrast in foliage and color, or for synchronous color, depending on the kind of garden you want.

Perennials as a group are the most versatile of all plants in the landscape. There are perennials that thrive in every type of soil from wet to dry, fertile to infertile, and in every exposure from full sun to shade. You can plant them alongside streams or in the dappled shade of trees, and naturalize the more vigorous ones in meadows, in the "wild garden," or in problem areas such as hillsides, steep embankments, and rocky outcroppings.

If you have an established low-maintenance landscape of trees and shrubs and want to add some seasonal color to relieve the year-round sameness of the scene, perennials are the perfect way to do it without having to replant annuals every year. Many gardeners are surprised to find that adding even a few perennials to a dull landscape can transform it into an attractive garden.

Because perennials are long-lived they are usually thought of as permanent plantings, but they needn't always be planted with that quality in mind. Like annuals, they can be used as *temporary* fillers among shrubs and trees or to brighten up dull or vacant spots in the yard. Unlike annuals, however, if a time comes when they have to be removed, most can easily be transplanted elsewhere. It's possible, in fact, to use other parts of the yard as "holding areas" for perennials until time to plant them in the flower garden.

As versatile and effective as perennials are in difficult or unconventional situations, it is in the flower garden that they are truly outstanding. Year after year they can provide beautiful flowers and foliage over a long season, from early spring until late fall. They are solid, reliable plants, and the feeling of permanence and stability they bring to the garden gives deep satisfaction and a welcome sense of security to every gardener.

Gardening has been popular throughout history, so much so that it has been developed, particularly in the form of the perennial border, into a genuine art. Later in this book there will be some examples of the glory the perennial border has reached through the efforts of some famous, extraordinarily skilled gardeners. This section examines the basic principles that will enable you to understand and create your own beautiful gardens with perennials.

The Cottage Garden

The best place to begin learning to design a garden is with the garden that shows the least design of all: the cottage garden. The English cottage garden, using the same plants as its more formal counterparts but without any particular plan or reason, was the forerunner of the most beautifully designed perennial beds and borders.

Cottage gardens are essentially the gardens of people who love plants for themselves and care little or nothing for the way they are organized. Plants are added according to the taste and whim of the gardener, and the only guiding principle is to have close at hand all of those plants the gardener

The true cottage garden looks as if it just happened without any planning by the gardener. But even this type of garden has some thought behind it. The cottage garden style is an important key to many aspects of perennial gardening and is referred to throughout this book. The English garden above includes pink lupines, old-fashioned climbing roses, blue delphiniums, and yellow Jerusalem sage *(Phlomis fruticosa)*.

loves, without much regard for such rules as placing taller plants in back or leading up to bright colors with more subtle ones. The effect is likely to be kaleidoscopic, with an old climbing rose, a clump of daylilies, a mat of nasturtiums, a towering stand of hollyhocks, and spots of cottage pinks, basket-of-gold, veronica, poppies, and other plants all growing on their own, without much focus. They are gardens of surprises, where such accidents of nature as the encroaching of vigorous plants upon one another and the sudden appearance of plants the gardener doesn't recall planting are gratefully accepted. The true cottage garden has a wild and woolly look, but it is also a charming, engaging garden to lose oneself in.

It may be that this loose approach to gardening and garden design appeals to you more than the idea of laying out a plan. If you have no experience with design, the idea of sitting down and developing a plan for your garden may seem a little intimidating. Or perhaps it seems like too much effort, when, with any luck, a more random approach will produce a beautiful garden. Why, then, should you bother learning about design?

Above: This photograph shows the value of spot plantings. Imagine this corner without the daylilies.

Right: A cardinal rule of garden design is to place flower beds or borders where they can be readily admired. The back porch of this house in Connecticut is a favorite sitting place, so the garden was arranged accordingly.

Why Design?

The simple fact is that different gardens can have the same quantities of exactly the same plants, and some of these gardens will still be more attractive than others. In almost every case, the difference is that the most beautiful gardens are those with a strong underlying design or structure. The sense of order a plan provides is especially important in flower gardens. With flowering plants, the variations in sizes, shapes, colors, and textures always pose the possibility of ending up with a messy jumble, and one that means more work. But if the basic framework of the garden is strong, any combination of plants and flowers can be supported easily, without the fear of the garden's becoming chaotic.

Unfortunately, the planning stage is too often ignored by beginning gardeners. Their gardens tend to grow randomly, by bits and pieces, and if some order does emerge, it is more by luck than by conscious effort. In the long run, however, you will create a much more beautiful garden if you take time to draw up some type of overall plan. By the time your garden matures, this underlying design may not be as obvious as in the beginning, but the organization it provided will still be there.

Planning the Design

At the beginning of any truly successful garden, a thoughtful plan was devised and carried out. Such factors as the lawn size and shape, the paths and walkways, shrub borders, hedges, trees, statues, and background fences and walls were all considered, both individually and as contributors to the creation of a total scene.

There are basically five steps to designing the perennial garden:

☐ Determining the point from which the garden will be viewed most often.

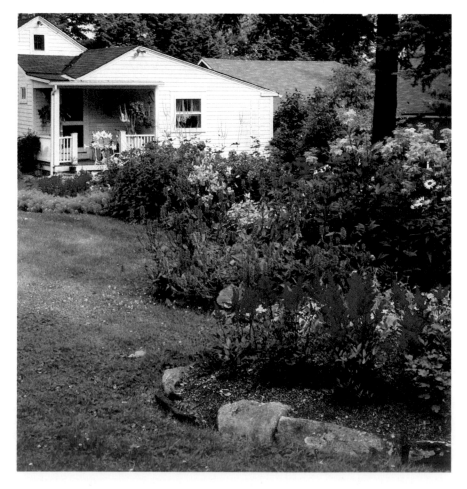

☐ Considering the shape and topography of your yard and which plants are there that are immovable or that you want to keep.

☐ Deciding whether you want a formal or informal design.

☐ Deciding whether you want beds or borders.

☐ Choosing your plants.

Viewpoint. The first step in planning your garden should be to determine from what angle or location it will most often be viewed. If you plan to view it primarily from inside the house, make sure to locate it so that you can see it comfortably through a favorite window. If you plan to spend a lot of time on a deck or patio, be careful to lay out the garden with that spot in mind.

Shape and topography. Once you know where to place the garden, the next step is to consider the shape and topography of your yard. This will in turn help you to decide whether to have a formal or informal design.

Formal or informal? If your yard is irregular, with slopes, hills, or rock outcroppings, or if there are mature trees or specimen plants that you wish to leave standing, you'll find it difficult to carry out a formal design. Such a site lends itself naturally to an informal plan, and most gardeners in these conditions will take that course. On the other hand, if your yard is flat with no outstanding natural features, you'll be free to choose whichever style you wish.

In the informal garden there is a predominance of curved flowing lines and a seeming disregard for symmetry. The curves of lawn areas, patios, walkways, beds, and borders are usually gentle, wide arcs frequently following the natural terrain. One curve should lead to another, creating a feeling of natural harmony.

Formal gardens are composed primarily of straight lines of classic symmetry; that is, what appears on the right side of the garden is matched,

A perennial garden of traditional formal design. Flanked by brilliant displays of flowers, the stone walkway leads to a pergola with a sitting area.

Right: If you have plenty of space, "island" flower beds make lovely displays. They can be viewed from all sides and are easily accessible for maintenance.

Borders allow more open space and are effective in either large or small gardens. If a border is so wide that tending background plants is difficult, a small path behind it will help.

sometimes nearly perfectly, on the left. The overall shape of the formal garden is frequently rectangular, and this shape is repeated in other parts of the plan, in pools, patios, and in flower beds and borders. Often a single object such as a statue, pool, or sundial serves as the center of interest, placed for optimum effect usually toward the rear of the garden, directly in the line of vision from the favorite viewing spot.

A formal garden is the easiest kind to lay out. Its visual simplicity can complement the right home and impart a special feeling to a small lot.

Once you have decided on the garden location and on a formal or informal plan, you want next to decide whether to plant beds or borders (or both, if you have the space).

Beds and borders. Beds and borders have been the key elements in garden design as long as there have been gardens. What are they exactly, and how do they differ? The term *bed* in this book refers to a cultivated area surrounded by an open expanse, usually a grass lawn. A border is a cultivated area that bounds or borders an expanse, such as a lawn, or adjoins a walkway. Beds and borders may be designed along either informal or formal lines.

Beds. For most of today's gardeners, the idea of a formal bed seems more suitable in a public park or on municipal grounds than in one's own back yard. Indeed, in the home garden beds are generally less popular and practical than borders for the simple reason that they should have fairly large open areas around them to look their best. Putting a bed into an average-size yard is like placing a table in the middle of an average-size room: it reduces the amount of free space substantially.

Still, beds have a number of important advantages. One strong proponent of informal beds, or "island beds," as he calls them, is Alan Bloom, one of the world's foremost authorities on perennials. Bloom favors beds for three reasons: first, because they are accessible from all sides they are easier to maintain than standard borders; second, they admit more sunlight and air circulation, which benefits the plants; and third, because they can be viewed from all sides, they hold more possibilities for the attractive arrangement of plants. If these features appeal to you and you have the space, beds may be ideal for your garden.

Borders. The greatest advantage of the border over a bed is that it takes up less space. If your yard is limited to the usual urban or suburban dimensions, there are good reasons for leaving the center open: to create the feeling of as much space as possible; to provide space for recreation; and to provide a "quiet" space to contrast with whatever visual activity you may have on the perimeter of the yard—trees, shrubs, or the flower border itself.

Much of the effectiveness of the border depends upon the open space it defines. There should be a pleasing relationship between the depth of the border (the distance from front to back) and the width of the yard. For example, if you want borders on each side of a yard 40 feet wide, borders 12 feet deep would create a "tunnel" effect. For the most pleasing proportion of borders and the space they enclose, the border depth should never exceed more than a quarter of the total width of the yard.

In addition to allowing more open space, borders soften the edges of buildings, fences, walkways, and lawns.

A border is often planted flush against a building or fence, which means it is accessible from one side only. This situation limits the border depth to about 5 feet; any more would make it difficult to tend plants in the back without walking on those in front. However, you can have a deeper border if you leave a space behind it at least 30 inches wide. The tallest plants will hide this rear path from view, but you will still be able to groom, prune, stake, and weed easily from that side. The path will also allow more of the air circulation plants need, and in addition it will make the border less vulnerable to invasion by the roots of shrubs or trees behind the border.

If you choose to plant a perennial border, you'll want to consider two other aspects of design: background and edging.

Backgrounds. For backgrounds, most of us must settle for whatever currently serves to separate our property from adjacent properties. This most often is a fence or wall, but may also be a hedge, shrubs, or, in part, buildings.

No doubt the most attractive backdrop for a secluded garden is a stone or brick wall. Next best is a weathered, natural wood fence. If you have a fence painted or stained an unappealing or difficult color, keep in mind that if you repaint or restain, you may have to do it again every few years. Try to choose

This planting extends out into the lawn, its elongated shape having the appearance of a border. Yet it also serves as an island bed because it can be tended and viewed from both sides.

Borders, more than beds, rely on an appropriate background. Here, the gardener has taken advantage of the rustic qualities of a stone wall.

paint closest to the color of the wood in its weathered state. Medium-to-dark earth tones make the best backgrounds for flowers.

If the fence is basically uninteresting, or if you have a chain link or wire fence or other structure that cannot serve as a backdrop, you can create a background by planting and training vines in a tracery pattern across the front. Wisteria, trumpet vine, lace vine, honeysuckle, and ivies are just a few possible choices.

Shrubs also make particularly attractive backgrounds. If you have room you may want to plant some, perhaps mixing evergreen and deciduous shrubs. Or you may want to plant a hedge. Needled evergreen hedges of such plants as yew generally grow much more slowly than broadleaf hedge plants such as privet. They take fewer nutrients from the soil, and thus their roots are much slower to invade the border. If planted as small plants, however, they may take 10 years or more to fill in completely.

A list of tall perennials suitable for backgrounds appears on page 35.

Edgings. Edgings serve to set off beds and borders from the surrounding yard. They also can discourage or prevent lawn grass or weeds from creeping into the planted area.

If the bed or border fronts onto a lawn, a row of bricks laid side-by-side and set slightly lower than the level of the turf will not only define the planting area but also make an excellent mowing strip. If your design is rectilinear, wood 2-by-4s or other lumber, even railroad ties, will make a strong edge. You will, however, have to edge the grass by hand where it meets the wood.

For a less formal look, fieldstones set in mortar can provide an attractive picture, especially if plants are allowed to drape and trail over them. You can also simply line stones along the edge, if you wish. And if a walkway flanks the bed or border, many people choose to have the first row of plants grow into it in a natural manner, as seen in the photograph. A list of perennials suitable for edging the border appears on page 35.

Another easy way to merely define the edge of a planting area is to install some of the small flexible wire fencing commonly available at garden centers.

Whatever you choose as your edging, remember that unless you provide some kind of underground barrier between the bed or border and the lawn, you'll be in for some extra weeding. Garden centers usually carry inexpensive rolls of metal or plastic strips for this purpose.

An important aspect of the flower bed or border is the edging. In this border featuring lilies and perennial grasses, railroad ties separate the planted area from the gravel walkway. Edgings can be fashioned from many materials that add beauty and make maintenance easier.

Choosing plants. Once you have gone through the previous steps in designing your garden, you're ready for that part of gardening that most people find the most fun of all—choosing your own plants. As you begin to make those choices, you may find it helpful to ask yourself these important questions:

☐ Are there any favorite plants that you really want or colors that you should not have because they would clash with or be overwhelmed by the color of a background wall, fence, or planting?

☐ Do you want one color scheme blooming all at once, or do you want a changing garden, with one wave of flowers giving way to the next?

☐ Do you want a diversity of plant and flower forms, or plants that are more or less similar in appearance?

☐ Does your space limit you to smaller plants, or can you accommodate some of the rangier ones?

Characteristics of Perennials

In designing the garden, there are several specific characteristics of perennials that you need to know in order to make the best choices. Obviously, the cultural requirements of the plants must match the soil, light, and climatic conditions in your garden. In addition, you need to note each plant's *color, height, spread, form, texture,* and *flowering season.* Let's look at each characteristic and the role it plays in garden design.

A standard color wheel.

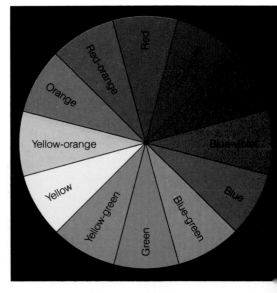

Color. Perennials come in a vast range of colors, so many that choosing can be confusing. However, understanding some simple principles of color can help you greatly in selecting flowers and blending them in the garden.

The color wheel on this page is a device showing the basic relationships among colors. For example, red, red-orange, orange, yellow-orange, and yellow are considered "warm" colors; green, blue-green, blue, blue-violet, and violet are considered "cool" colors. (Red-violet and yellow-green have both warm and cool properties, one more than the other depending upon what colors they are combined with.) Although colors are obviously neither warm nor cool in a physical sense, they can impart *feelings* of warmth or coolness, and of passion or tranquility.

To the eye, warm colors tend to advance and cool colors tend to recede: if planted side-by-side at a distance, the warm colors would appear closer, the cool colors farther away. You can use these effects to create spatial illusions.

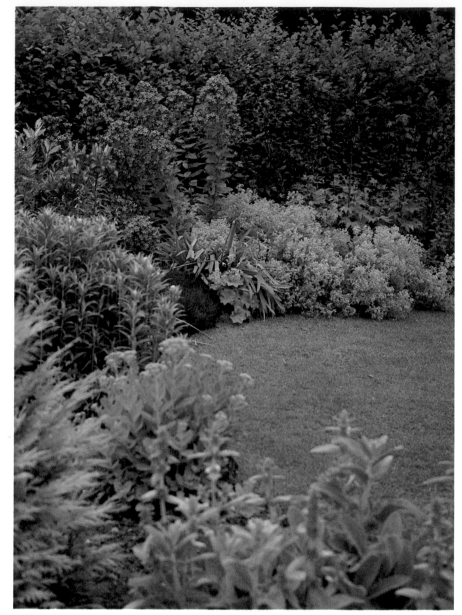

Right: This garden beautifully illustrates how cool colors tend to recede and warm colors advance toward the viewer. Although these plants are planted closely together, note how the lavender-blue phlox fades into the background while the darker blue delphiniums seem even farther away. The yellow-green gopher plant *(Euphorbia lathyrus)* has just enough yellow to stand out, and the warm orange lilies seem almost to be in the foreground.

Below: Many gardeners are especially fond of plants with silver and gray foliage. Shown here are the low-growing gray lavender cotton *(Santolina chamaecyparissus)* and green pygmy barberry, backed by the taller gray lamb's ears *(Stachys olympica)*.

A planting of predominantly cool-colored flowers at the rear of your garden would make the yard seem larger; warm colors would make it seem smaller. Spot plantings can have similar effects, making a part of the yard seem farther away or closer.

Generally, cool colors are good for close-up viewing and warm colors better for dramatic displays. Plantings of blue campanula, violet meadow sage, and purple phlox may have quite an impact next to the patio or walkway, but planted in the back of the garden they would have little effect. To emphasize cool colors, it's best to plant them closest to the point from which they'll be most often viewed. Warm-color plants such as red hibiscus, yellow heliopsis, and orange asclepias can be used to bring a distant part of the yard into sharp focus. When combining warm and cool colors, remember that the cooler colors can be easily overwhelmed by the warmer colors.

A pure color is called a *hue*. A *tint* is lighter than the pure color and a *shade* is darker. In combining hues, tints, and shades, there are four basic schemes:

Monochromatic schemes are those with flowers in various tints and shades of one color. No garden is truly monochromatic, of course, because the

Two monochromatic color schemes. At the far left are shades of red in dahlias, petunias, tuberous begonias, and pelargoniums. The dark purple foliage in the background is smoke tree (*Cotinus coggygria* 'Notcutt's'). At the left are shades of pink in *Sedum spectabile* (foreground), *Monarda* 'Croftway Pink' (middle ground), and pink cosmos (background).

Two analogous color schemes. At the far left are *Stachys officinalis* (foreground), sweet William and cosmos (middle ground), and *Cirsium japonicum* (background). At the left are achillea (foreground), helianthus (right), and rust-colored rudbeckia (background).

Two complementary color schemes. At the far left are yellow *Aurinia saxatile* and purple scilla. At the left are *Allium senescens* (foreground), yellow rudbeckia, and white *Achillea millefolium* 'Emerald Isle'.

PLANNING A PERENNIAL GARDEN / 23

This planting at Healing Garden in England is a superb example of a polychromatic color scheme, and indeed of all the elements of perennial border design. It is a skillful combination of colors, plant forms and sizes, foliage textures, flower shapes, and timing of flowering.

green of foliage is always present; but flowers in tints and shades of one color can be particularly harmonious and attractive, and the idea is certainly worth trying. Many gardeners use this scheme to complement the color of their house.

Analogous schemes use colors closely related to one another on the color wheel. Any three adjoining colors are said to be analogous; for example, red, red-violet, and violet. These schemes have been used in creating some of the world's most beautiful gardens. On page 61 you will see the famous "tonal" garden of Vita Sackville-West, based on rules quite similar to those for the analogous scheme.

Complementary schemes combine colors opposite one another on the wheel; for example, red and green, yellow and violet, and orange and blue. These are powerful combinations, clashing to some, vibrant and vital to others. They are best with pure colors, or hues, rather than shades or tints. If you want to try to "blend" strong complementary colors, arrange them to intermingle where they meet rather than be clearly defined. To tone these colors down you can include silvery-leaf or white-flower plants. If you want to plant intensely colored flowers like scarlet red Oriental poppies, clear yellow rudbeckias, or hot pink Michaelmas daisies, you can always lead up to the bright spots with plants of similar but less intense colors. Beds and borders designed according to this principle have a pleasing rhythm and cohesion to them.

Polychromatic schemes often produce a gay, carnival-like atmosphere in the garden. They may combine any and every color. Such gardens are often the result of random plantings, particularly by the novice gardener. There is nothing wrong with this, assuming the gardener didn't have something else in mind, and in fact it can lead to some happy surprises—accidental but especially pleasing color combinations that become the mainstay of the garden for seasons to come.

These principles should be helpful in choosing flower colors for your garden. You'll find lists of perennials arranged by color on pages 36–38. Foliage color is also a consideration. Perennials come with foliage in all shades and tints of green, in blue-green, blue-gray, silvery blue, silvery gray, gray, and in many variegations. Generally, it's a good idea when designing to avoid plants with variegated foliage: they are notoriously difficult to combine with flowers. Plants with silver or gray foliage, however, have been the pets of many gardeners. Dusty miller, santolina, lamb's ears, and verbascum are just some of the silver- or gray-foliage plants that produce striking effects when combined with flowers, particularly white flowers or flowers in the pale blue to lavender range of the spectrum.

Height. Perennials range in height from under a foot to as much as 12 feet. The standard rule for borders is to stair-step the plantings from the tallest in the rear to the shortest in front. In island beds of mixed plantings, the tallest obviously should be near the center. If these rules are followed strictly, however, the result is likely to be too static. Some variations in the rules will allow for a more natural effect and a more attractive garden, as long as plants aren't actually obscured from view. Lists of perennials arranged by height appear on page 35.

Spread. The spread of a plant at maturity is an extremely important factor in planning a garden, one that unfortunately is commonly overlooked by gardeners. Newly planted beds or borders, if planted with the correct spacing between plants, naturally look a little sparse, with more soil than plant showing. In the eagerness for a lush, full garden, the temptation is to fudge a little (or a lot) and space the young plants closer together than recommended. Although it may seem a nuisance to look up the spread of each plant and allow for it in your plan, if you do not do it you will eventually discover new meaning to the word "nuisance" by having to deal with a jammed-up formless jungle of plants all competing for light, water, and nutrients. If you do allow them enough room to grow, you'll be glad you did.

Form. Plants have their own forms, and these too are important design considerations. For all practical purposes, there are five basic growth forms in herbaceous plants; *rounded, vertical, open, upright and spreading,* and *prostrate.* Some gardens are composed of only one form; others alternate and repeat certain forms. Many outstanding beds and borders are made up of complementary forms, mixing the rounded with the vertical. If you have some difficulty in considering form for your design, it may help to imagine the garden in silhouette. Lists of perennials by form appear on pages 35–36.

Although their characteristics are too subtle to play a great role in design, you may want to think about flower forms. The forms that perennial blooms take are too numerous and complex to enumerate, but some are: the bell-shaped campanulas, dishlike shasta daisies or asters, spherical peonies, cup-shaped marsh marigolds, spurred columbines, frilly or lacy dianthus, star-shaped amsonia, and trumpetlike daylilies. Flowers may also be borne singly at the ends of stems, in clusters, or in spikes.

The daisy family is so large that gardeners frequently find themselves with an overabundance of the daisy shape. Generally, the most interesting gardens are those that offer some contrast in flower forms.

Texture. When we speak of the texture of plants, we mean the textural *appearance* of the plant, not the way it feels to the touch. Plants may be said to be *coarse, medium,* or *fine* in texture. Texture is determined by such factors as how dense the foliage is, the form of the plant, and how close the flowers are to one another. For example, the plume poppy is coarse in texture, the peony medium, and artemisia fine.

Like color, texture can be used to create spatial illusions in the garden. Coarse-textured plants will appear closer, and fine-textured plants will recede into the distance. This is useful, for example, with a long, narrow border. If you wish to make the far end seem closer, you can do so by planting coarse-textured plants at that end. Plants with a fine texture can make a shallow border appear deeper.

Flowering season. The most important single aspect of perennial gardening is timing bloom. To design with perennials you must know when each plant will flower and for how long. Different perennials bloom at different times throughout the season and for different periods of time. (Some, of course, do coincide.) These factors must be coordinated to produce the effects you want. And this is the most challenging, most interesting, and most exciting feature of perennial gardening.

This coordination is necessary because, although there are many exceptions, perennials generally bloom for two to four weeks, a shorter duration than annuals, which generally bloom over a long season. To extend the period of color, you must select plants with varying flowering times or durations of bloom. (If faded flowers are cut back, most perennials will bloom again. This second flowering will produce more, but smaller, flowers.)

Of course, you may want to select flowers that do bloom at approximately the same time for a garden filled with color. This is fine if you want a spectacular display at a particular time and are willing to settle for little or no perennial bloom the rest of the season. Or you may want a longer duration of color and plant for a continuous succession of flowers, with new flowers appearing as others fade. This will have a diluting effect on the overall garden color; but it will also reveal something more of the forms of the plants. In general, even when you plant for a succession of bloom, there will be three or four peak periods of flowering during the season, interspersed with less colorful periods of quietude.

While it may be difficult to envision these changing patterns, a time lapse film of a perennial border taken from early spring to late summer would clearly show one wave of flowers replacing another. On pages 32–33 is an excellent example in pictures of how a perennial garden changes through the growing season.

To help you pick perennials for a succession of bloom, the chart on page 27 illustrates how they relate to one another in time and duration of flowering season.

With varying time and duration of flowering, the possibilities of the perennial garden are immense. When you add the job of coordinating color to coordinating these two factors, the possibilities become even more immense, so great that they may seem overwhelming to the beginning gardener. The question might be raised, why bother with all this, why not merely plant annuals when and where you need them for a full season of bloom? The simple answer, apart from the uniquely attractive characteristics and longer life of the perennials, is that the perennial garden planned for a succession of bloom is always changing, and thus is not one garden, but many gardens in one.

The Plant Selection Guide starting on page 64 is an ideal way to find out a great deal about many different perennials in a short time. It lists all of the previously mentioned characteristics—cultural requirements, color, height, spread, form, texture, and flowering season—for each plant. The lists beginning on page 35 will help you choose plants for different characteristics and cultural conditions. You'll find additional sources for plants and plant information on page 41. As you learn more about the

Flowering Chart

	JAN	FEB	MAR	APRIL	MAY	JUNE	JULY	AUG	SEPT	OCT	NOV	DEC
Helleborus niger	■	■										
Helleborus lividus var. corsicus		■	■									
Helleorus orientalis			■	■	■							
Aurinia saxatilis					■							
Bergenia cordifolia					■							
Brunnera macrophylla					■							
Mertensia virginica					■							
Phlox subulata					■							
Primula vulgaris					■							
Primula × polyantha					■							
Primula sieboldii					■							
Pulmonaria saccharata					■							
Pulmonaria angustifolia					■							
Euphorbia epithymoides					■	■						
Iris, Bearded						■						
Aquilegia						■						
Caltha palustris						■						
Dianthus plumarius						■						
Doronicum cordatum						■						
Euphorbia cyparissus						■						
Geranium sanguineum						■	■					
Geum hybrids						■						
Iris, Pacific Coast						■						
Paeonia hybrids						■						
Polygonatum commutatum						■						
Primula japonica						■						
Stachys grandiflora						■						
Trollius europaeus						■						
Acanthus mollis						■						
Amsonia tabernaemontana						■						
Baptisia australis						■						
Dicentra eximia						■	■					
Dicentra spectabilis						■						
Dictamnus albus						■						
Hemerocallis hybrids						■	■	■				
Alchemilla vulgaris						■						
Anchusa azurea						■	■					
Asclepias tuberosa						■	■					
Astilbe							■					
Campanula glomerata							■					
Campanula carpatica							■					
Chrysanthemum coccineum							■					
Chrysanthemum × superbum							■					
Coreopsis lanceolata							■					
Coreopsis verticillata							■					
Delphinium elatum							■					
Digitalis purpurea							■					
Filipendula hexapetala							■					
Gaillardia × grandiflora							■	■				
Arrhenatherum elatius (a grass)							■					
Heuchera sanguinea							■					
Kniphofia uvaria							■	■				
Lupinus 'Russell hybrids'							■					
Lychnis chaledonica							■					
Lychnis × haageana							■					
Lysimachia nummularia							■					
Lysimachia punctata							■					
Papaver orientalis							■					
Penstemon hartwegii							■					
Salvia pratensis							■					
Salvia × superba							■					
Scabiosa caucasica							■	■				

	JAN	FEB	MAR	APRIL	MAY	JUNE	JULY	AUG	SEPT	OCT	NOV	DEC
Thermopsis caroliniana							■					
Tradescantia virginiana							■					
Veronica incana							■					
Veronica latifolia							■					
Iris sibirica							■					
Achillea							■					
Aruncus dioicus							■					
Chrysogonum virginianum							■	■				
Cimicifuga racemosa							■					
Coreopsis grandiflora							■					
Filipendula rubra							■					
Filipendula ulmaria							■					
Deschampsia caespitosa (a grass)							■	■				
Iris kaempferi							■					
Monarda didyma							■					
Veronica hybrids							■					
Anthemis tinctoria							■					
Campanula persicifolia							■					
Chrysanthemum parthenium							■					
Echinacea purpurea							■					
Echinops exaltatus							■					
Euphorbia corollata							■					
Schizachyrium scoparium (a grass)										■	■	■
Gypsophila							■					
Heliopsis helianthoides							■	■				
Hosta sieboldiana							■					
Hosta undulata							■					
Hosta ventricosa							■					
Liatris							■					
Lysimachia clethroides							■					
Lythrum salicaria							■					
Platycodon grandiflorus							■					
Stachys officinalis							■					
Stokesia laevis							■					
Thalictrum rochebrunianum							■					
Veronica longifolia							■					
Veronica spicata							■					
Belamcanda chinensis								■				
Helenium autumnale								■	■			
Hibiscus moscheutos								■				
Lobelia cardinalis								■				
Phlox paniculata								■				
Rudbeckia								■				
Salvia azurea								■				
Stachys byzantina								■				
Aconitum napellus								■				
Aster								■	■			
Ceratostigma plumbaginoides								■				
Chrysanthemum hybrids									■	■	■	
Cortaderia selloana (a grass)									■	■		
Molinia caerulea (a grass)									■			
Helianthus decapetalus								■				
Hosta fortunei								■				
Hosta decorata								■				
Hosta lancifolia								■				
Ligularia dentata								■				
Sedum spectabile								■	■			
Solidago hybrids									■			
Anemone × hybrida									■	■		
Miscanthus sinensis (a grass)										■	■	
Hosta plantaginea									■			
Hosta tardifolia									■			

individual plants, it's good to keep a list of those you think may be good for your garden, so that you'll have it handy when you begin laying out your plan on paper.

Mapping the Garden

Assuming you have gone over the design basics and have chosen or are in the process of choosing your plants, you may be ready to start drawing up a garden plan.

Graph paper will allow you to get the most realistic picture of your space and proportions. It is easy to work with paper with four squares to the inch, allowing each square to represent 1 square foot of garden space.

First, outline on the paper the shapes of your beds and borders. Then

Upper right: Subtlety is the key to this border. The lower-growing *Hosta* and *Pulmonaria* are planted at the front, and the tall *Thalictrum* at the back.

Below: Sequence of bloom is the key intention of this border plan. Low-growing *Festuca* and *Heuchera* are in front, and the taller *Heliopsis* and *Miscanthus* are at the back.

A Garden That Changes with the Season

The border plan below offers change and progression, from bulbs and peonies through summer blossoms and winter grasses. *Festuca* and *Heuchera* provide an evergreen edging. The other plants, including peonies and iris, display good foliage during all growing seasons.

In May, the peonies blossom. Their flowering overlaps that of the Siberian irises, which peak in June along with the *Heuchera*, as the *Geum* and *Heliopsis* begin to flower.

Geum and *Heliopsis*, with long flowering seasons from late June through August, share the garden with *Rudbeckia*, which peaks in late July and into August, and *Sedum*, which blooms in August.

By early July, the grasses have gained good height. They flower, then seed in mid-August and into winter. Their seeds and foliage color and that of *Rudbeckia* and *Sedum* provide interest until spring.

Except for *Heliopsis* and *Festuca*, which perform best with yearly division, the plants in this garden require low maintenance.

For unity and added color, fragrance, and texture, underplant with long-lived bulbs, such as narcissus, and seed in forget-me-nots.

Plant list
The number in brackets following each entry is the number of plants you will need for this 6-by-20-foot border.
Festuca ovina 'Glauca' (Blue Fescue); silvery blue, evergreen foliage [54]
Geum 'Mrs. Bradshaw' (Avens); red [7]
Grasses: *Miscanthus sinensis* 'Gracillimus' (Eulalia Grass); pinkish or silvery plumes [10]
Pennisetum alopecoroides (Fountain Grass); coppery tan flowers [6]
Heliopsis helianthoides (Heliopsis); yellow [8]
Heuchera sanguinea (Coral Bells); pinks and whites [50]
Iris sibirica (Siberian Iris); blue [12]
Paeonia hybrids (Peony); pinks and whites [5]
Rudbeckia fulgida 'Goldsturm' (Goldsturm Black-eyed Susan); yellow with black [40]
Sedum spectabile (Showy Sedum): pinks and whites [14]

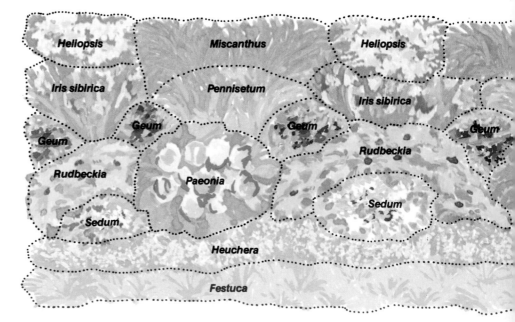

from a numbered list of your plant choices, insert the numbers on your plan. If you wish, you can insert information on any of the plant characteristics, whatever might give you a better picture of the garden. You can use any designations you want for these characteristics; for example, *T, M,* and *S* (for tall, medium, or short) might be used for height; *CT, MT,* or *FT* might be used for coarse, medium, and fine texture. Some gardeners find it helpful to use colored pencils to indicate color. And if you are planning for a succession of bloom, you can use overlaying layers of tracing paper to indicate how the garden will appear at different times of the year.

Your plan can be as simple or complex as you like, and you can draw as many as you like. When you happen upon a scheme you prefer, you'll know it.

We've chosen two sample plans to illustrate the process.

A Textural Border for a Shady Spot

The border at left is designed for a moist, shady area. The plants in it were chosen for their understated qualities of foliage and texture or their ability to accentuate those qualities. Form and color of foliage and flower shape may play an even more effective role than flower color, which serves primarily as accent.

In zone 6, flower color will be most apparent from late June to early July, with the exception of the early-blooming *Pulmonaria* and *Aquilegia. Astilbe, Aruncus, Cimicifuga,* and *Thalictrum* blossoms lend a feathery texture to the border. *Astilbe, Cimicifuga,* and *Hosta* add a spikey quality.

The play of foliage against foliage enlivens the garden in all seasons. *Cimicifuga, Astilbe,* and *Aruncus* echo one another in the similarity of their complicated, compound leaves, with textures ranging from medium to bold.

The simple variegated and various-colored cabbagelike leaves of *Hosta* and *Pulmonaria* range from gray to light and dark green, in medium to very bold textures.

Both *Aquilegia* and *Thalictrum* have fine, soft-textured, grayish foliage resembling maidenhair fern.

Plant list
The number in brackets following each entry is the number of plants you will need for this 6-by-10-foot border.
Aquilegia (Columbine); mixed blue, yellow, pink [4]
Aruncus dioicus (Goatsbeard); white [2]
Astilbe hybrids (False Spirea); whites and pinks [10]
Cimicifuga racemosa (Bugbane); white [4]
Hosta, mixed
   H. plantaginea (Fragrant Plantain Lily); white [4]
   H. lancifolia (Narrow-Leaf Plantain Lily); pale lilac [4]
   H. ventricosa (Blue Plantain Lily); pale lilac [4]
Hosta sieboldiana (Blue-Leaf Plantain Lily); pale lilac [2]
Hosta undulata (Wavy-Leaf Plantain Lily); pale violet [8]
Pulmonaria saccharata (Bethlehem Sage); blue, reddish violet [5]
Thalictrum rochebrunianum (Lavender Mist Meadowrue); lavender [4]

Some of the best flower gardens include a mixture of annuals and perennials. Here the perennial *Rudbeckia fulgida* provides bright yellow contrast to annual pansies, red snapdragons, pink geraniums, chrysanthemums, and white nicotiana.

The Mixed Border

When you choose plants for the perennial border, by no means are you limited to perennials only. In fact, if what you want is a fairly steady blaze of color, you'll have to add other plants, because that can't be provided by perennials alone.

Perennials do have the advantage of being permanent additions to the border, and thus provide the basic framework; but for the most part the warm-season annual flowers have a longer blooming season. This makes them indispensable for color during "quiet" periods in the garden or to succeed faded perennial bloom.

Many of the most beautiful flower beds and borders in the world have predominately perennial plants, but annuals, bulbs, flowering shrubs, and many other plants are equally important parts of the scene. If you limit yourself to perennials alone, you'll miss out on such powerful color combinations as pink coral bells and orange California poppies, orange nasturtiums and blue salvia, and rich purple heliotrope with dark rose penstemon.

Spring- and summer-flowering bulbs are also important to any flower border, if only for the variety of unusual flower shapes they provide: daffodils in many varieties, grape hyacinths, fritillaria, tulips, and crocus are just a few of the spring-blooming bulbs that add excitement to the border well in advance of most perennial and annual bloom. The mid-summer border can be made more interesting by adding any of the lily hybrids, the cactus-flowered dahlias, nerine, gladioli, and the many varieties of allium.

The main drawback to an all-perennial border is that it is bare in winter. If you include a few hardy shrubs or small trees, you'll have something to look at during the cold months to testify that there is indeed a garden under all that snow or rain-soaked earth. When choosing shrubs and small trees for the border, it's best to pick those that will not overgrow their allotted space; and to look for varieties with some interesting fall or winter characteristics, such as bright foliage, berries, or an attractive branch pattern when the plant is bare. Such trees include dwarf forms of crabapple or flowering cherry, Japanese maple, or the flowering chestnut. Dwarf hollies, the tree peonies, dwarf junipers, and varieties of hebe are only a few of the shrubs that are restrained in growth.

A cutting garden can provide plenty of your favorite flowers for indoor use. The owner of this one favors many varieties of long-stemmed chrysanthemums.

The Cutting Garden

If you're a person who enjoys the beauty of cut flowers indoors, you may want to consider setting aside a small bed primarily for an old-fashioned cutting garden.

Perennial flowers are among the most prized of all cut flowers, lending themselves particularly to large, striking arrangements. A dozen or so red-hot pokers in a tall glass cylinder, masses of blue delphiniums in a copper kettle, or a combination of sunflowers and coreopsis in a rustic wicker container are just a few possibilities.

Because the cutting garden is basically utilitarian, it should be laid out in a simple, practical manner. The plants can be planted in rows like a vegetable garden, with the tallest set so they won't shade the lower-growing varieties. A seldom-used sideyard is an ideal place for a cutting garden as long as it receives at least a half day of sun. The soil should be properly prepared.

Cut flowers will keep longer if you follow a few simple rules. Generally, it's best to cut flowers in the morning or evening when they are most turgid with water; flowers cut in the middle of the day are somewhat wilted and once cut will have difficulty absorbing water.

Always use a sharp knife or pair of scissors to make the cleanest cut possible. Take a pail of warm water into the garden and plunge the stems into it immediately after cutting.

When arranging the flowers remove any foliage from the base of the stems to discourage bacterial growth in the water in the vase. Professional flower arrangers often cut the stems again before putting the flowers into the vase. For the longest life, they advise cutting stems underwater and making the cut at an angle. Conditioning the flowers before they are arranged by placing the cut stems in water and refrigerating them for 4 to 6 hours will also make them last longer.

Arrangements will hold up best in a cool room away from direct sunlight. Change the water daily to promote the longest life. Cut flower "foods" available at some garden centers and florists can be added to the water to prolong the blossoms.

Cutting gardens also serve as excellent places to hold perennials in reserve until you want to plant them in the landscape or garden.

A list of perennials that make outstanding cut flowers can be found on page 40.

Perennials can make excellent container plants. This unusual arrangement includes statice, ivy geranium, and ivy.

Perennials in Containers

Perennials can make excellent container plants, especially when combined with annuals or bulbs. Such plantings provide a much longer season of color and a good contrast between foliage and flowers. As the early bulbs and perennials pass their prime, the annuals can fill in and cover with a summer-long display of flowers.

Some combinations of annuals, perennials, and bulbs that you might want to try are: dark pink penstemons and a lighter pink 'Cascade' petunia; perennial blue salvia with blue trailing lobelia; 'King Alfred' daffodils with basket-of-gold; and the bushy 'Connecticut Yankee' delphinium, blue hyacinths, white sweet alyssum, and 'Blue Mariner' petunias.

Container culture. From a design point of view, containers offer the advantage of mobility. You can group containers around the patio or deck or at an entryway, adding color where you like and changing the color schemes and patterns as you wish. Containers also can serve as holding areas for flowers you may wish to plant in the garden later.

Garden centers, nurseries, and variety stores offer wide selections of containers in all sizes: clay and ceramic pots, wooden half-barrels, and plastic and wood pots and boxes. Experienced container gardeners favor the largest containers possible: the bigger they are, the more soil they hold, which means less watering for the gardener, more root space for the plants, and more room to experiment with different combinations of plants.

If you use clay pots, it's a good idea to wet them down thoroughly before planting. Clay is very porous and absorbent and if dry will quickly rob newly planted plants of their first soaking. Cover the drainage hole (or holes) with broken pieces of pottery, irregularly shaped stones, or a small piece of fine-mesh screen. (It is not necessary to provide additional drainage with a layer of gravel or stones on the bottom.)

You can fill the containers with garden soil *if* your soil is a good loam with excellent drainage. If you've had problems growing plants in your soil, you'll only intensify the problems when you use it in containers. Repeated waterings tend to compact soil to the point where there is very little air space left, making drainage very slow. If your soil is marginally acceptable, mix it in equal proportions with an organic soil amendment such as peat moss, compost, or redwood soil conditioner, to make it a lighter, looser growing medium more conducive to growing plants in confined quarters. If your soil is actually poor, you'll be better off using one of the prepackaged soil mixes sold under a variety of brand names such as Jiffy Mix, Redi-Earth, Metro Mix, Super Soil, Pro-Mix, and many others.

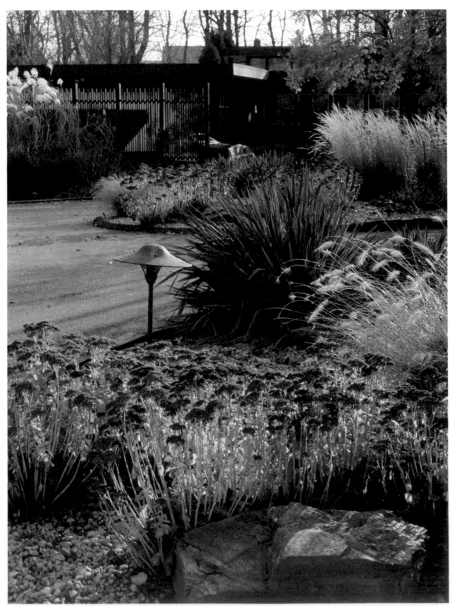

Two photographs of the same garden, designed by Oehme, van Sweden & Associates, show the scene in late fall and early summer. The primary plantings are *Sedum spectabile*, fountain grass, plume poppies, and pampas grass. Comparably beautiful in both seasons, this type of landscaping exemplifies a new trend in designing with perennials.

Before planting, thoroughly water the soil mass and allow it to settle. After settling, there should be enough space between the rim and the soil so that *one* watering will moisten the rootball and drain through. If the container is too full of soil, the job becomes time-consuming and aggravating, requiring several waterings for a complete soaking.

Because of the limited amount of soil available, plants in containers need more attention than plants in the open ground. During the hot summer months, daily watering is commonly needed, especially if the containers are in a sunny or windy location. These repeated waterings leach nutrients out of the soil rather quickly. To compensate for this loss, most container gardeners favor applying balanced liquid fertilizers at half-strength every 2 weeks.

To keep specimens looking their best, be sure to pinch off any dead flowers or leaves regularly.

A New Look for Perennials

It's often said that there is nothing really new in gardening; and it is certainly true that most new trends in gardening tend to be a revival of some sort, a rediscovery of a form of gardening from the past. In recent years

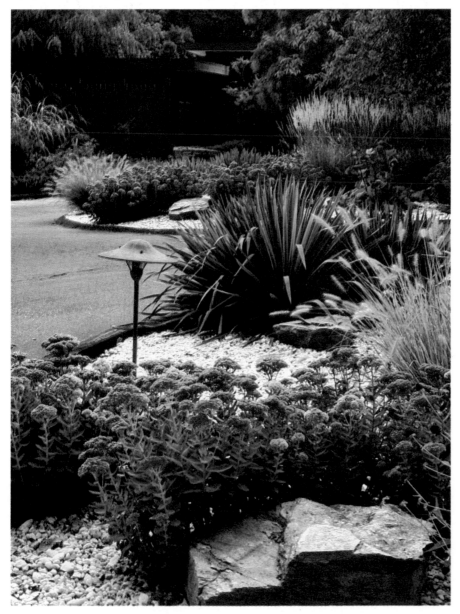

though, the landscape architecture firm of Oehme, van Sweden & Associates in Washington, D.C., has designed a number of dramatic gardens, the likes of which have not been seen before. The plants are certainly not new, but the way they are being used and the aesthetics behind the garden design are fresh and different enough to constitute a new form of gardening.

The governing concept behind these gardens is the creation of a low-maintenance landscape using masses of a limited number of different plants, the majority of which are perennials. But they don't resemble anything like the English perennial border—rather than emphasizing flower combinations, these gardens are carefully thought out displays of contrasting textures and forms, with a subtle use of color that changes constantly with the seasons.

A garden by Oehme, van Sweden & Associates might start out in early spring with a massive display of naturalized daffodils or grape hyacinths, all bulbs that can remain undisturbed for years and which multiply in the process. These are followed in early summer by the lush new growth of black-eyed Susans (*Rudbeckia hirta*), *Sedum spectabile*, fountain grass (*Pennisetum setaceum*), eulalia grass (*Micanthus sinesisis* 'Gracillimus'), and plume poppies (*Macleaya* species). In midsummer the black-eyed Susans begin to bloom in what can only be described as a huge outdoor bouquet (see the illustration), followed shortly by the plume poppies. In late summer the grasses start to send up their feathery plumes, followed by the flowering sedum. The sedum flowers start out pale greenish-white and, as the weather turns progressively cold, change from pink to a deep dusky rose.

Instead of trimming off all the spent flowers and dried leaves, the architects leave the plants intact through the first hard frosts and snow. What remain are the dried leaves of the grasses, with their tall, bare seed spikes, the dark seed heads of the black-eyed Susans, and the by now bronze flowers of the sedum, just before they disappear under a blanket of snow. One of the principals in the firm says the winter garden looks like an oversize dried arrangement of flowers and leaves.

These unique gardens dramatically illustrate the extraordinary creative possibilities in designing with perennials.

This garden by Oehme, van Sweden & Associates was photographed in midsummer. Although most of the grasses have not yet begun to flower, the mass planting of black-eyed Susans creates a strong effect.

Perennial Performers

The following lists of perennials are categories according to height, form, color, application to special problems, and use. The lists can be an invaluable tool for the gardener who needs to organize many different elements into a cohesive whole. Use them to spark your imagination or to solve landscaping problems. Keep in mind that, in many cases, when a name appears on a list, only selected varieties (usually too numerous to mention in the list) may fit the given category. Consult the Plant Selection Guide, seed catalogs, and local experts to help pinpoint the variety most suited to your needs.

Large perennials

Large perennial plants provide a general effect of mass with their dense foliage serving as backdrop to a border. An asterisk (*) indicates that the plant may reach a height of 5 feet or more.

Aruncus dioicus (Goatsbeard)
Baptisia australis (False Indigo)
Cortaderia selloana (Pampas Grass)
Delphinium elatum (Delphinium)
Helianthus decapetalus (Sunflower)
Hibiscus moscheutos (Rose Mallow)
Macleaya cordata (Plume Poppy)
Miscanthus sinensis (Eulalia Grass)
Schizachrium (Little Bluestern)
Thalictrum rochebrunianum (Lavender Mist Meadowrue)
Thermopsis caroliniana (False Lupine)

Low perennials

Low perennial plants grow to no more than 18 inches in height and are useful in the front of a border, for edging, or in front of taller, leggy plants. Those marked with an asterisk (*) have the additional quality of spreading by forming mats or trailing across the ground and are useful in beds or as groundcovers.

Achillea ptarmica (Yarrow)
Alchemilla (Lady's Mantle)
Armeria (Sea Pink)
Artemisia (Wormwood)
Aster, selected varieties (Aster)
Aurinia (Basket-of-Gold)
Bergenia (Bergenia)
Brunnera (Siberian Bugloss)
Campanula carpatica (Carpathian Harebell)
Ceratostigma (Blue Plumbago)
Chrysanthemum × morifolium (Hardy Chrysanthemum)
Chrysanthemum parthenium (Feverfew)
Chrysogonum (Golden Star)
Dianthus (Pink)
Elymus (Blue Lyme Grass)
Festuca (Blue Fescue)
Gaillardia (Blanket Flower)
Geranium (Cranesbill)
Gypsophila repens (Creeping Baby's Breath)
Hakonechloa macra, a grass
Heuchera (Coral Bells)
Hosta (Plantain Lily)
Iris, dwarf bearded (Dwarf Bearded Iris)
Lysimachia nummularia (Moneywort)
Oenothera missourensis (Ozark Sundrops)
Phlox subulata (Moss Pink)
Primula (Primrose)
Pulmonaria (Lungwort)
Sedum (Stonecrop)
Tiarella (Foam Flower)
Trollius (Globe Flower)

Form: Vertical accent

The plants listed include those with an overall vertical form and with spikey or nonspikey flowers, and those with only spikey flowers.

Acanthus (Bear's Breech)
Astilbe (False Spirea)
Baptisia (False Indigo)
Cimicifuga (Bugbane)
Cortaderia (Pampas Grass)
Delphinium (Delphinium)
Digitalis (Foxglove)
Iris (Iris)
Kniphofia (Torch Lily)
Liatris (Blazing Star)
Ligularia dentata 'The Rocket' (Golden Groundsel)
Lobelia cardinalis (Cardinal Flower)
Lupinus (Lupine)
Miscanthus (Eulalia Grass)
Nepeta (Catmint)
Penstemon (Beardtongue)
Primula japonica (Japanese Primrose)
Salvia (Sage)
Schizachyrium (Little Bluestem)
Stachys grandiflora (Big Betony)
Thermopsis (False Lupine)
Veronica (Speedwell)
Yucca (Spanish Bayonet)

Form: Rounded

The following plants have a smoothly rounded, bushy habit of growth and are dense, in general, with foliage from top to bottom.

Artemisia (Wormwood)
Aruncus (Goatsbeard)
Baptisia (False Indigo)
Chrysanthemum parthenium (Feverfew)
Chrysanthemum × superbum (Shasta Daisy)
Coreopsis verticillata (Threadleaf Coreopsis)
Deschampsia (Tufted Hair Grass)
Dicentra (Bleeding Heart)
Dictamnus (Gas Plant)
Erigeron (Fleabane)
Euphorbia (Spurge)
Festuca (Blue Fescue)
Gaillardia (Blanket Flower)
Geranium (Cranesbill)
Gypsophila (Baby's Breath)
Helenium (Sneezeweed)
Helictotrichon (Blue Oat Grass)
Heliopsis (Heliopsis)
Hemerocallis (Daylily)
Hosta (Plantain Lily)
Paeonia (Peony)
Platycodon (Balloon Flower)
Sedum spectabile (Showy Stonecrop)
Thermopsis (False Lupine)

Form and texture play a strong role in this garden, highlighted by the feathery texture of astilbe blossoms and the spikey flowers and rounded foliage of hosta.

Form: Open

The plants in this list have an open, loose form. They are best displayed when mixed and interplanted with other perennials in a border.

Aquilegia (Columbine)
Echinacea (Coneflower)
Echinops (Globe Thistle)
Eryngium (Sea Holly)
Helianthus (Sunflower)
Linum (Blue Flax)
Lychnis coronaria (Rose Campion)
Papaver (Poppy)
Scabiosa (Pincushion Flower)
Thalictrum (Meadowrue)
Tradescantia (Spiderwort)

Flower Color: The Yellow Range

These plants include varieties with flowers in the color range from yellow-green; and yellow to orange and bronze.

Achillea (Yarrow)
Alchemilla (Lady's Mantle)
Anthemis (Golden Marguerite)
Aquilegia (Columbine)
Asclepias (Butterfly Flower)
Aurinia (Basket-of-Gold)
Caltha (Marsh Marigold)
Chrysanthemum (Chrysanthemum)
Coreopsis (Calliopsis)
Delphinium (Delphinium)
Digitalis (Foxglove)
Doronicum (Leopard's Bane)
Euphorbia (Spurge)
Gaillardia (Blanket Flower)
Geum (Avens)
Helenium (Sneezeweed)
Helianthus (Sunflower)
Heliopsis (Heliopsis)
Helleborus (Christmas Rose)
Hemerocallis (Daylily)
Iris (Iris)
Kniphofia (Torch Lily)
Ligularia (Groundsel)
Lupinus (Lupine)
Lychnis (Campion)

Lysimachia nummularia (Moneywort)
Lysimachia punctata (Yellow Loosestrife)
Oenothera (Evening Primrose; Sundrop)
Paeonia (Peony)
Papaver (Poppy)
Penstemon (Beardtongue)
Primula (Primrose)
Rudbeckia (Black-eyed Susan)
Solidago (Goldenrod)
Thermopsis (False Lupine)
Tradescantia (Spiderwort)
Trollius (Globe Flower)

Flower Color: The Whites

These plants include varieties with flowers in the color range from white to cream.

Acanthus mollis (Bear's Breech)
Achillea ptarmica (Yarrow)
Aconitum (Monkshood)
Anthemis (Golden Marguerite)
Aquilegia (Columbine)
Armeria (Sea Pink)
Aruncus (Goatsbeard)
Aster (Aster)
Astilbe (False Spirea)
Bergenia (Bergenia)
Campanula (Harebell)
Chrysanthemum (Chrysanthemum)
Cimicifuga (Bugbane)
Delphinium (Delphinium)
Dianthus (Pink)
Dicentra (Bleeding Heart)
Dictamnus (Gas Plant)
Digitalis (Foxglove)
Echinacea (Coneflower)
Filipendula (Queen of the Prairie)
Geranium (Cranesbill)
Gypsophila (Baby's Breath)
Hemerocallis (Daylily)
Heuchera (Coral Bells)
Hibiscus (Rose Mallow)
Hosta (Plantain Lily)
Iris (Iris)
Kniphofia (Torch Lily)
Liatris (Blazing Star)
Lupinus (Lupine)

Lysimachia clethroides (Gooseneck
    Loosestrife)
Monarda (Bee Balm)
Paeonia (Peony)
Papaver (Poppy)
Penstemon (Beardtongue)
Phlox (Phlox)
Polygonatum (Solomon's Seal)
Primula (Primrose)
Stokesia (Stokes' Aster)
Thalictrum (Meadowrue)
Tiarella (Foamflower)
Tradescantia (Spiderwort)
Veronica (Speedwell)
Yucca (Spanish Bayonet)

Flower Color: The Red Range
These plants include varieties with flowers
in the color range from red to pink
and pinkish-purple.

Achillea millefolium 'Fire King' (Fire King
    Yarrow)
Aquilegia (Columbine)
Armeria (Sea Pink)
Aster (Aster)
Astilbe (False Spirea)
Bergenia (Bergenia)
Campanula (Harebell)
Chrysanthemum coccineum (Painted Daisy)
Chrysanthemum × morifolium (Hardy
    Chrysanthemum)
Cortaderia (Pampas Grass)
Delphinium (Delphinium)
Dianthus (Pink)
Dicentra (Bleeding Heart)

Dictamnus albus 'purpureus' (Rose Gas
    Plant)
Digitalis (Floxglove)
Erigeron (Fleabane)
Filipendula (Queen of the Prairie)
Gaillardia (Blanket Flower)
Geranium (Cranesbill)
Geum (Avens)
Gypsophila (Baby's Breath)
Helleborus (Christmas Rose)
Hemerocallis (Daylily)
Heuchera (Coral Bells)
Hibiscus (Rose Mallow)
Iris (Iris)
Kniphofia (Torch Lily)
Liatris (Blazing Star)
Limonium (Hardy Statice)
Lobelia (Cardinal Flower)
Lupinus (Lupine)
Lychnis (Campion)
Lythrum (Purple Loosestrife)
Macleaya (Plume Poppy)
Monarda (Bee Balm)
Paeonia (Peony)
Papaver (Poppy)
Pennisetum (Fountain Grass)
Penstemon (Beardtongue)
Phlox (Phlox)
Platycodon (Balloon Flower)
Primula (Primrose)
Pulmonaria (Lungwort)
Scabiosa (Pincushion Flower)
Sedum (Stonecrop)
Thalictrum (Meadowrue)
Tradescantia (Spiderwort)
Veronica (Speedwell)

Daylilies *(Hemerocallis)* have attractive
foliage and a wide range of brilliant colors.
They are excellent cut flowers and are
admirably suited to all climates.

Beautiful color and a strong upright effect distinguish this combination of *Iris sibirica, Thalictrum aquilegifolium, Lychnis chalcedonica,* and *Dictamnus albus.*

Flower Color: The Blue Range

These plants include varieties with flowers in the color range from blue and violet to lavender and bluish-purple.

Aconitum (Monkshood)
Amsonia (Blue Star)
Anchusa (Bugloss)
Aster (Aster)
Baptisia (False Indigo)
Brunnera (Siberian Bugloss)
Campanula (Harebell)
Ceratostigma (Blue Plumbago)
Delphinium (Delphinium)
Echinacea (Coneflower)
Echinops (Globe Thistle)
Eryngium (Sea Holly)
Geranium (Cranesbill)
Hosta (Plantain Lily)
Iris (Iris)
Limonium (Hardy Statice)
Linum (Blue Flax)
Lupinus (Lupine)
Mertensia (Virginia Bluebells)
Phlox (Phlox)
Platycodon (Balloon Flower)
Polemonium (Jacob's Ladder)
Primula (Primrose)
Pulmonaria (Lungwort)
Salvia (Sage)
Scabiosa (Pincushion Flower)
Stachys (Betony)
Stokesia (Stokes' Aster)
Tradescantia (Spiderwort)
Veronica (Speedwell)

Cool-summer Lovers

These perennials are best when grown in climate zones that have cool summers, such as mountainous or coastal regions.

Aconitum (Monkshood)
Aquilegia (Columbine)
Astilbe (False Spirea)
Delphinium (Delphinium)
Dicentra (Bleeding Heart)
Ligularia (Groundsel)
Lupinus (Lupine)
Penstemon (Beardtongue)
Primula (Primrose)
Thalictrum (Meadowrue)

Best for the South

All of the following plants will perform well as far south as USDA zone 9. Those marked with an asterisk (*) are well adapted to zone 10.

*Acanthus (Bear's Breech)
Achillea (Yarrow)
Amsonia (Blue Star)
Anthemis (Golden Marguerite)
Armeria (Sea Pink)
Artemisia (Wormwood)
Aruncus (Goatsbeard)
Asclepias (Butterfly Flower)
Baptisia (False Indigo)
Bergenia (Bergenia)
Brunnera (Siberian Bugloss)
Campanula (Harebell)
Ceratostigma (Blue Plumbago)

Chrysanthemum (Chrysanthemum)
Coreopsis (Calliopsis)
Dicentra (Bleeding Heart)
Digitalis (Foxglove)
Echinacea (Coneflower)
Echinops (Globe Thistle)
Erigeron (Fleabane)
Eryngium (Sea Holly)
Euphorbia (Spurge)
Filipendula (Queen of the Prairie)
Gaillardia (Blanket Flower)
Geum (Avens)
Grasses: All. *Cortaderia* (Pampas Grass)
Helianthus (Sunflower)
Heliopsis (Heliopsis)
Helleborus lividus var. *corsicus* (Corsican Hellebore)
Hemerocallis (Daylily)
Heuchera (Coral Bells)
Hibiscus (Rose Mallow)
Hosta (Plantain Lily)
Iris (Iris)
Kniphofia (Torch Lily)
Liatris (Blazing Star)
Limonium (Hardy Statice)
Linum (Flax)
Lychnis (Campion)
Lythrum (Loosestrife)
Macleaya (Plume Poppy)
Mertensia (Virginia Bluebells)
Monarda (Bee Balm)
Oenothera (Evening Primrose; Sundrops)
Penstemon (Beardtongue)
Phlox (Phlox)
Platycodon (Balloon Flower)
Rudbeckia (Black-eyed Susan)
Salvia (Sage)
Scabiosa (Pincushion Flower)
Sedum (Stonecrop)
Sempervivum (Hen-and-Chickens)
Solidago (Goldenrod)
Stachys (Betony)
Stokesia (Stokes' Aster)
Tradescantia (Spiderwort)
Veronica (Speedwell)
Yucca (Spanish Bayonet)

Tolerant of dry soil

These perennials will tolerate drought and poor, dry soil better than most.

Achillea (Yarrow)
Amsonia (Blue Star)
Anthemis (Golden Marguerite)
Armeria (Sea Pink)
Artemisia (Wormwood)
Asclepias (Butterfly Flower)
Aurinia (Basket-of-Gold)
Baptisia (False Indigo)
Chrysanthemum parthenium (Feverfew)
Cortaderia (Pampas Grass)
Coreopsis (Calliopsis)
Dianthus (Pink)
Echinops (Globe Thistle)
Elymus (Blue Lyme Grass)
Erigeron (Fleabane)
Eryngium (Sea Holly)
Euphorbia (Spurge)
Festuca (Blue Fescue)
Gaillardia (Blanket Flower)
Geranium (Cranesbill)
Hemerocallis (Daylily)
Iris, Pacific Coast varieties (Pacific Coast Iris)
Kniphofia (Torch Lily)
Liatris scariosa (Tall Gayfeather)
Limonium (Hardy Statice)

Linum (Flax)
Miscanthus (Eulalia Grass)
Nepeta (Catmint)
Rudbeckia (Black-eyed Susan)
Salvia (Sage)
Schizachyrium (Little Bluestem)
Sedum (Stonecrop)
Solidago (Goldenrod)
Stachys (Betony)
Thermopsis (False Lupine)
Tradescantia (Spiderwort)
Yucca (Spanish Bayonet)

Tolerant of moist soil

The following perennials are good choices for that difficult low, soggy spot in the garden.

Aruncus (Goatsbeard)
Caltha (Marsh Marigold)
Cimicifuga (Bugbane)
Filipendula (Queen of the Prairie)
Hibiscus (Rose Mallow)
Iris kaempferi (Japanese Iris)
Iris pseudacorus (Yellow Flag)
Lobelia cardinalis (Cardinal Flower)
Lysimachia (Loosestrife)
Lythrum (Purple Loosestrife)
Mertensia (Virginia Bluebells)
Monarda (Bee Balm)
Primula japonica (Japanese Primrose)
Tradescantia (Spiderwort)
Trollius (Globe Flower)

For the shade

Some of the following plants tolerate shade, many actually prefer it. For most shade lovers, the light, filtered shade of high tree limbs is ideal. Those marked with an asterisk (*) are tolerant of deeper shade. Remember that no plant will survive long in deep, black darkness.

Acanthus (Bear's Breech)
Aconitum (Monkshood)
Alchemilla (Lady's Mantle)
Anemone (Anemone)
Aquilegia (Columbine)
Aruncus (Goatsbeard)
Astilbe (False Spirea)
Bergenia (Bergenia)
Brunnera (Siberian Bugloss)
Campanula (Harebell)
Ceratostigma (Blue Plumbago)
Chrysogonum (Golden Star)
Cimicifuga (Bugbane)
Dicentra (Bleeding Heart)
Digitalis (Foxglove)
Doronicum (Leopard's Bane)
Euphorbia (Spurge)
Filipendula (Queen of the Prairie)
Hemerocallis (Daylily)
Heuchera (Coral Bells)
Hosta (Plantain Lily)
Iris sibirica (Siberian Iris)
Ligularia (Groundsel)
Lobelia cardinalis (Cardinal Flower)
Lysimachia (Loosestrife)
Macleaya (Plume Poppy)
Mertensia (Virginia Bluebells)
Monarda (Bee Balm)
Polemonium (Jacob's Ladder)
Polygonatum (Solomon's Seal)
Primula (Primrose)
Pulmonaria (Lungwort)
Thalictrum (Meadowrue)
Tiarella (Foamflower)
Trollius (Globe Flower)

This landscape features magenta *Geranium psilostemon* in the foreground with *Mimulus lewisii* at the upper right and a stand of old roses.

Cut flowers

Not all of the perennials useful for cut flowers will be found in this list, only some of the best. The flowers of those plants marked with an asterisk (*) are especially suitable for drying and preserving.

Acanthus (Bear's Breech)
Achillea (Yarrow)
Anemone (Anemone)
Anthemis (Golden Marguerite)
Aster (Aster)
Chrysanthemum (Chrysanthemum)
Coreopsis (Calliopsis)
Delphinium (Delphinium)
Dianthus (Pink)
Digitalis (Foxglove)
Echinacea (Coneflower)
*Echinops (Globe Thistle)
Eryngium (Sea Holly)
Gaillardia (Blanket Flower)
Geum (Avens)
Grasses: All.
*Gypsophila (Baby's Breath)
Helenium (Sneezeweed)
Helianthus (Sunflower)
Heliopsis (Heliopsis)
Hemerocallis (Daylily)
Heuchera (Coral Bells)
Hosta (Plantain Lily)
Iris (Iris)
Kniphofia (Torch Lily)
Liatris (Blazing Star)
Limonium (Hardy Statice)
Lupinus (Lupine)
Nepeta (Catmint)
Paeonia (Peony)
Papaver (Poppy)
Rudbeckia (Black-eyed Susan)

Scabiosa (Pincushion Flower)
*Solidago (Goldenrod)
Stokesia (Stokes' Aster)
Veronica (Speedwell)

Attractive foliage

The following plants are especially valuable for their foliage effect. The notation (C) signifies a coarse, bold texture; (M) a medium texture; and (F) a fine texture. The notation (G) indicates gray or silvery foliage, and (E) indicates that the plant is evergreen. Many plants that are evergreen in warmer climates may be only semievergreen the farther north they are grown.

Acanthus (C) (Bear's Breech)
Alchemilla (M) (Lady's Mantle)
Amsonia (F) (Blue Star)
Armeria (F, E) (Sea Pink)
Artemisia (F, G) (Wormwood)
Aruncus (C) (False Spirea)
Aurinia (G) (Basket-of-Gold)
Baptisia (M) (False Indigo)
Bergenia (C, E) (Bergenia)
Coreopsis verticillata (F) (Threadleaf
    Coreopsis)
Dianthus (F) (Pink)
Eryngium (G) (Sea Holly)
Euphorbia (M) (Spurge)
Grasses: All.
Helleborus (E) (Christmas Rose)
Hemerocallis (E, selected varieties) (Daylily)
Heuchera (E) (Coral Bells)
Hosta (C) (Plantain Lily)
Iris kaempferi (M) (Japanese Iris)
Iris sibirica (M) (Siberian Iris)
Kniphofia (M) (Torch Lily)
Ligularia (C) (Groundsel)

Macleaya (C) (Plume Poppy)
Nepeta (G) (Catmint)
Paeonia (M) (Peony)
Polemonium (M) (Jacob's Ladder)
Polygonatum (M) (Solomon's Seal)
Pulmonaria (M) (Lungwort)
Salvia × superba (G) (Perennial Salvia)
Sedum (M) (Stonecrop)
Sempervivum (M) (Hen-and-Chickens)
Stachys byzantina (G) (Woolly Betony)
Thalictrum (F) (Meadowrue)
Tiarella (M) (Foamflower)
Yucca (G) (Spanish Bayonet)

Fragrance

Some of the more fragrant perennials are included in the list below. An asterisk (*) indicates that the plant foliage is fragrant when crushed or bruised.

*Achillea (Yarrow)
*Anthemis (Golden Marguerite)
*Artemisia (Wormwood)
Cimicifuga (Bugbane)
Dianthus (Pink)
Dictamnus (Gas Plant)
Filipendula (Queen of the Prairie)
Hemerocallis (selected varieties) (Daylily)
Hosta plantaginea (Fragrant Plantain Lily)
Iris, bearded (Bearded Iris)
*Monarda (Bee Balm)
Oenothera (Evening Primrose; Sundrops)
Paeonia (Peony)
Phlox paniculata (Garden Phlox)
Primula (Primrose)
*Salvia (Sage)

A selected list of major suppliers for perennial plants and catalogs

Alpenglow Gardens
13328 King George Highway
Surrey, B.C., CANADA

Bluestone Perennials
7203 Middle Ridge Road
Madison, OH 44057

Carroll Gardens
Westminster, MD 21157

Garden Place
6780 Heisley Road
Mentor, OH 44060

Klehm Nursery
2 E. Algonquin Road
Arlington Heights, IL 60005

Lamb Nurseries
E. 101 Sharp Ave.
Spokane, WA 99202

Rakestraw's
G—3094 South Term Street
Burton, MI 48529

Spruce Brook Nursery
Route 118
Box 925
Litchfield, CT 06759

Wayside Gardens
Hodges, SC 29695

White Flower Farm
Litchfield, CT 06759

Gilbert H. Wild & Sons
Sarcoxie, MO 64862

Salmon-colored Oriental poppies and white and pink peonies make an attractive blend in this border.

BASIC CARE AND CULTURE

Like all plants, perennials have certain climatic, soil, and maintenance requirements. A good working knowledge of these is fundamental to success with perennials.

Perennials, like most plants, require only the basics for good growth: a reasonably fertile soil, good drainage, sufficient sun and water, and a little tender loving assistance from the gardener.

This section gives you the principles of these basics. It tells you step by step how to evaluate your soil and bring it into excellent condition for perennials. It also tells you where to find the plants you want and, for those interested in economy and a rewarding gardening venture, how to start your own perennials from seed. It also covers transplanting, staking, fertilizing, watering, pest and disease control, and it even tells you how to divide the plants—in short, just about everything you need to know to grow healthy, vigorous perennials.

Soil Preparation

Some areas of the country have naturally occurring "good soil" that requires little attention from the gardener. These soils have plenty of organic matter, ample nutrients, and a structure that allows good air and moisture circulation and a strong foothold for roots.

If this is your soil, count yourself blessed, because there's nothing quite like already having quality soil to garden in with no effort needed to make it that way. But if you're not so fortunate, don't gamble on trying to garden without improving your soil. Nothing is so disappointing as having to deal with a difficult soil that produces minimum success and a multitude of problems.

The best time to prepare your soil for perennials is at least a couple of months before you intend to plant. This waiting period allows any amendments you add to the soil to take effect. Most perennials are planted in fall or spring; so soil should be prepared in the summer for fall planting, or in the fall for spring planting.

The first quality to look at in your soil is its texture. The two extremes in texture are clay and sand. Clay consists of microscopic particles bound too closely together to allow much drainage or root penetration. Sand does not retain enough moisture and drains so quickly that nutrients are leached out. If your soil has too much sand or clay, it will also have a poor structure, meaning that it will not form the crumblike particles needed by most plants for good growth. Both clay and sand, however, have their virtues, and in the right combinations make excellent soils.

There is a simple test for texture and structure that gardeners have used for centuries. First take a shovel or cultivator and work up the soil a bit; then take a handful, squeeze it in your palm, open your hand and see what happens. If the soil holds together for a few seconds, and then crumbles apart, you have a good-quality soil known as a loam soil. If it just sits in your hand in one big lump, it either has too high a clay content or is too wet. If the weather has been fairly dry, you know that your soil has too much clay, and

you'll want to improve it. If the soil doesn't adhere to itself but flows through your fingers, you know it's too sandy and will need some work. (Note that this test is also a good one to see if your soil is dry enough to cultivate or to plant.)

Improving Your Soil

Improving soils that are too clayey or sandy is an easy task: you merely add organic matter—and plenty of it—into the top layer. Organic matter is simply material that was once a living plant and adding it is the best thing you can do for your soil. It holds water and nutrients like a sponge, increasing the soil's capacity for both; it opens and loosens the soil; and as it breaks down into *humus* (the dark, decayed substance that gives soil its characteristic color), it forms gluelike materials that stick soil particles together in little crumbs, forming a soft, rich medium perfect for good root growth. Such a loose soil of good structure and texture is called a *friable* soil.

Almost all organic materials are good for your soil, and there are many available. They include those you can find at most nurseries and garden centers, such as shredded bark, chunk bark, leaf mold, peat moss, and manures; and those that you produce yourself or get from other sources, such as sawdust, hay, lawn and garden clippings, weeds, corncobs, and compost.

How much organic matter to add depends upon the condition of your soil and the depth to which you want to condition it. If your garden has been growing healthy plants, or even a healthy weed crop, and if you've noticed no drainage problems such as water from rain or sprinklers puddling up, you may not need to add much. Generally, it's almost impossible to add too much organic matter, and any amount you do add will improve the soil quality. (Extremely soft, fluffy, acid soils that are mostly organic matter are an exception.) One widely observed rule of thumb is to add an amount equal to one-third to one-half the depth of soil you want to condition; for example, a 2- to 3-inch layer over 6 inches of soil, a 4- to 6-inch layer over 12 inches of soil, and so on.

If the organic matter is not completely decayed and does not already have added nitrogen (if it does, the label will say "nitrogen-fortified"), you'll need to add some. Two pounds of ammonium sulfate (or the equivalent) per 100 square feet will prevent the organic matter from robbing the soil of the nitrogen that decay bacteria need to break it down further.

With many clay soils, another amendment of great value is gypsum. Gypsum helps to improve the structure of clay soils. It should be added at a rate of about 5 pounds per 100 square feet. If it works, drainage will be improved almost immediately. Extremely heavy clay soils are another problem entirely, and in some cases cannot by any means be made into good soil. If you suspect that you have one of these soils, before you go to the expense of trying to improve it, contact your local nurseryman or County Extension Agent for more information.

Soil pH

At the same time you test the texture and structure of your soil, it's a good idea to check its pH. Many states offer free or low-cost pH tests (for details call your County Extension Agent); or, you probably can find inexpensive testing kits at your local garden center. The test is easy to perform.

The letters *pH* stand for the chemical term *potential hydrogen*, which is a measure of acidity and alkalinity. The pH scale runs from 0, extremely acid, to 14, extremely alkaline, with the middle of the scale, 7, the neutral point. The vast majority of perennials grow best in neutral or slightly acid soils.

If your soil is extremely acid, you can add ground limestone to correct it. If alkalinity is a problem, you can correct it by adding garden sulfur or

Testing the pH of your soil is easy and can help you build excellent soil. Simple pH test kits such as this can be found in most garden centers.

ferrous sulfate. Both are available at nurseries and garden centers. Ask your nurseryman or County Extension Agent for the specific rates to apply. You will need to know the present pH of your soil, the type of soil you have, and what pH level you are trying to achieve.

Fertilizer

At the same time you add organic matter and lime or sulfur to the soil, it's good to add a complete fertilizer as well. Packaged dry fertilizers are the easiest to apply. Choose a formulation such as 5–10–5, one that is high in phosphorus and relatively low in nitrogen. (The numbers refer to the percentages of nitrogen, phosphorus, and potassium, in that order.) Apply it at about 3 to 5 pounds per 100 square feet. A fertilizer high in nitrogen content will stimulate leafy growth at the expense of flowers. Phosphorus stimulates both root growth and the formation of flowers. Potassium, or potash, contributes to stem strength and increases resistance to disease.

Cultivating the Soil

If the simple hand test mentioned earlier indicated that your soil is ready to be worked, the first step is to clear the site of all weeds. It's far better to pull the weeds out by hand than to hoe or scrape them off, which may leave roots that may grow back. The next step is to turn the soil over, being careful to remove any remaining weed roots: the spade or rototiller will chop these up if you don't get them and in effect multiply the number of weeds you'll have to deal with later.

After the site is clear of weeds, spread the organic matter, fertilizer, and, if needed, the lime or sulfur, all in a more or less even layer on top. Small amounts of any amendment will not change the soil structure appreciably; so spread the organic matter around with a free hand. If you're using peat moss, be sure it is moist when you take it from the bag. If not, moisten it with warm water while it is still in the bag, or use a wetting agent especially made for this purpose, available at garden centers.

In small areas, the easiest way to prepare your soil is by hand. For larger beds you may want to use a power tiller.

Now you are ready to work the soil. For some gardeners, this means using a shovel, spade, or digging fork to turn the top layer, breaking it into smaller pieces as they go. Those with fairly large gardens use a rototiller. One method is not necessarily better for the soil than the other, but if you are using a rototiller, keep these points in mind: first, don't overdo it; a couple of passes should make a good planting bed and any more may make the soil so fine that the first application of water will produce a thick crust on the soil surface. Second, most rototillers are limited in the depth they can cultivate, usually to 6 to 8 inches. It is generally believed that the deeper you cultivate the soil for perennials (and this is especially true with heavy clay soils), the better will be your results. If you want to produce the best possible planting bed, you will have to cultivate by hand. And you may want to use the method known as "double-digging."

Double-digging. Double-digging involves digging the top 10 or so inches of soil and moving it to a holding area. You then spade the subsoil layer, working organic matter into it as you go, to a depth of another 10 inches or so. Finally, you amend the topsoil with organic matter and fertilizer and layer it on top of the improved subsoil.

The only practical way to double-dig a bed is to do it in strips, as shown in the illustration. It is a laborious job that requires much effort and patience, and this is not everybody's cup of tea. Many knowledgeable gardeners point out that since most of the feeder roots of perennials are in the top layer of the soil, cultivating 6 to 8 inches deep is quite enough to produce healthy, vigorous plants. Still, double-digging produces an excellent planting bed that can remain untouched for years afterward and offers the advantage of drought resistance because of deeper root development.

Double Digging

Double-digging is a laborious, time-consuming technique of cultivation but produces excellent results. First, strip the top layer of soil to a depth of about 10 inches, then cultivate the subsoil to a similar depth, adding in organic matter. Amend the top layer and replace it. Double-dug beds have been known to stay in superb condition for many years.

Power tillers. If you prefer to use a power tiller to incorporate the amendments into the soil, remember that the heavier the machine, the easier the work. Power tillers are available for rental in most communities.

Make sure the soil is sufficiently moist, but not wet, before you begin. If not, water the soil thoroughly, then wait a few days to let it dry out somewhat before you start tilling. If your soil is unusually heavy, it may take several passes with the tiller to cultivate the soil to a depth of 6 inches; but remember not to overcultivate the soil. After cultivating, use a large metal rake to smooth the surface in preparation for planting.

Plant Sources

The fact that perennials have been the favorite plants of generations of gardeners is good testimony to their value in any present-day garden. It is the legacy of these gardeners that today there are literally thousands of varieties of perennials to choose from, a selection to keep the most ambitious gardener content for a lifetime.

After you have decided what style of planting you want—bed, border, plants simply spotted through the landscape, or container plants—you will want to make up a plant list. You can compile the list from the Plant Selection Guide (starting on page 64), from other books, from garden catalogs, or from plants you have seen growing in other gardens or at a local nursery or garden center.

The best sources for plants are nurseries and garden catalogs, but don't fail to consider plants given by or exchanged with gardening friends. As perennials outgrow their allotted spaces, they need to be divided, and divisions from established plants are generally as good as those available from nurseries and catalogs. It's good to remember, though, that any plant that has outgrown a neighbor's garden probably will do the same in yours. Plants most frequently handed over the back fence are usually the most vigorous and invasive ones. It's best to think twice about where you plant them, and allow plenty of room for expanding growth.

Nurseries. If you're fortunate, you'll have a nursery close by that handles a good selection of perennials. These most often will be climatically adapted to your region. And a large nursery or garden center probably will offer perennials in several different stages of development.

More and more nurseries are offering perennials as first-year seedlings planted in flats or plastic containers called "cell packs" or "six packs." These may take another year of growth in the garden to produce a good display of flowers, but the price represents a considerable saving over those in 4-inch pots or gallon cans.

You'll see the greatest selection of potted perennials at your nursery during their season of bloom, the spring and summer months. Obviously it is much easier to sell plants as an "impulse item" when they are in full bloom; but this is also an aid to the novice gardener who doesn't mind spending the extra money to see exactly what he or she is getting.

When choosing nursery plants, try to select those that are bushy and compact; avoid any that are sparse and leggy. A healthy green leaf color is a good sign that the plants have been well cared for. It's tempting to pick out plants that are in full bloom, but plants without flowers are usually more satisfactory in the long run. Also, fresh stock is usually preferable to plants that have been growing in small containers for many months. It's a good idea to find out the days the nursery receives its shipment from the whole-sale grower. If you're there when the truck is unloaded, not only will you get the freshest plants, but you'll also be able to pick from the widest selection.

Catalogs. If the selection of perennials is limited at your local nursery or garden centers, you'll need to rely on ordering from catalogs or starting your own perennials from seed. The list on page 41 contains many reputable sources for seeds and plants. Some of the catalogs feature perennials almost exclusively; others include other garden plants. If you are looking for hard-to-find varieties, the specialty catalogs are best.

If there is a charge for the catalog, it is usually nominal, and most companies refund its cost with your first order. Some companies print two catalogs: a spring selection and a fall selection The spring catalog (the one most companies offer, and the one that most excites gardeners) is mailed in the winter; the fall catalog is usually sent out in the spring. This gives gardeners a chance to make their choices and have the plants shipped at the proper planting time.

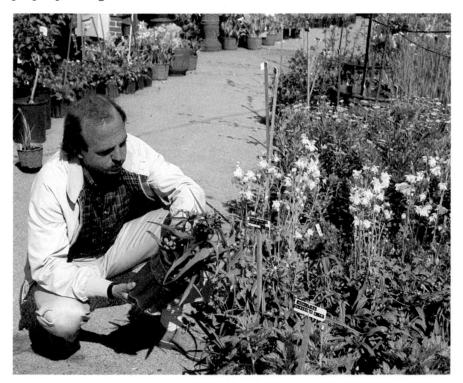

Most large nurseries and garden centers carry a good selection of perennials in gallon cans. Many of these will be in bloom. Plants this size are comparatively expensive, but they allow the gardener to see exactly what the foliage and flowers look like before planting, and also provide a head start on growth.

Live perennials ordered from catalogs usually arrive one of two ways: as dormant, bare-root plants with roots enclosed in damp sphagnum moss, wrapped in plastic; or as potted plants with the top growth visible. Companies generally are careful to note where the order is being sent and will wait to ship until the weather there is suitable for planting.

Catalogs serve another extremely important function for the gardener: to sit down with a catalog filled with enticing descriptions and colorful illustrations, especially when the garden outside is in a state of winter drabness, is pure pleasure and a great inspiration toward the new gardening season.

Starting Your Own

Starting your perennials from seed is an intriguing and rewarding venture, if you have the patience and the room to try it. Planting seed has several advantages, not the least of which is that it is the least expensive way to procure a large number of plants. Another benefit is that you are not limited to the varieties offered at your local nursery, or to those available as plants from mail-order sources. Selections offered by nurseries that specialize in perennials often include rare varieties you may want to try.

Always buy the best quality seeds you can find, and plant them the year you receive them: the freshest seeds give the best results. Some perennials are particular about the conditions they need in order to germinate. Read the instructions included with the seeds carefully and do your best to provide the conditions called for. The Plant Selection Guide, starting on page 64, includes instructions for those perennials it lists with unusual seed-starting requirements.

Over a period of time, gardeners develop their own favorite methods for starting seeds. The following is one way that works well for many perennials.

Getting started. The equipment should include a number of seed flats or trays with drainage holes, a top-quality growing medium such as *milled* sphagnum moss (not to be confused with peat moss), heating cables to provide warm soil (if necessary), and some type of fluorescent light unit whose height above the flats can be adjusted.

First, moisten the milled sphagnum in a plastic bag or other container, place it in the flats, and firm it down slightly to form a smooth, even surface. You can scatter the seeds over the surface, or plant them in rows. Sow the seeds thinly, tapping them out of the packet slowly for an even spread.

The next steps depend upon the specific requirements of the seeds. Some need light and heat to germinate and others require darkness and fairly cool temperatures. Some have periods of dormancy that need to be overcome by chilling in the refrigerator. Some seeds, in order to germinate most quickly, need to be soaked or to have their seed coats filed. Be sure to check closely the instructions that come with the seeds.

Moisture is critical in seed germination, and it's best not to take chances. The best way to supply moisture is to water from the bottom, not the top. You can place the flat or tray in the sink or in a larger pan, such as a cookie sheet, pour water into the sink or pan, and allow it to seep up into the soil. To maintain humidity, it's best to place a sheet of clear plastic over seeds that need light to germinate, and a sheet of black plastic over those that need darkness. Be sure, however, to remove the plastic as soon as the seeds start to sprout; otherwise, you'll be risking fungus disease that can wipe out the seedlings.

Maintaining moisture is especially critical with very fine, dustlike seeds, which have a tendency to dry out quickly.

Transplanting seedlings. Once the seeds have germinated and have produced their second set of true leaves, they are ready to be planted into their own containers. Small peat pots are best, as these can be planted directly into the garden. Fill them with good-quality packaged soil mix and wet it down before you start to transplant, and be careful not to let the seedlings dry out between the time you remove them from the flat and the time they are safely in the new containers.

Transplanting requires patience and dexterity. A flat pointed stick such as an old plant label works well to separate the seedlings and to ease them into the new soil. Use a light touch when firming the new soil around the roots of seedlings; too much pressure will squeeze the air from the soil, making it an unhealthy medium for the tender plants.

Many perennials do not take well to transplanting. Seeds of these should be sown directly into peat containers.

Seedlings in containers should be kept in a protected environment such as a lath house or cool greenhouse for several weeks. After they are established they can be moved to a somewhat less protected environment; but they are still not ready for full exposure to the elements. They will need more or less constant watering during warm summer months, and applications of an all-purpose complete fertilizer every 4 to 6 weeks throughout the growing season to get them on their way. Within a year's time you should have quite a collection of healthy, good-size perennials ready to go into the garden.

Perennial seeds of course can be sown directly into the garden, but with varying degrees of success and usually a very low percentage of germination. Following the previous instructions will greatly increase germination and allow you to control your supply of plants.

Transplanting Dormant Plants

If you ordered dormant plants from a catalog, they should arrive sometime in early spring. They won't look like much, but they are alive and should be treated with care. If the weather does not permit planting immediately, keep them in a cool, dark spot and make sure the sphagnum moss surrounding them doesn't dry out.

When the time comes to plant them in the garden, remove them from their plastic coverings, shake the moss off carefully, and inspect the roots.

To plant dormant plants, remove any plastic wrapping from the rootball and carefully shake loose the packing material.

Inspect the roots. Remove any that are dry and brittle or appear to have rotted.

Without wasting any time, position the dormant plant in the hole so that the crown is at soil level. Backfill with soil and remove any air pockets, using gentle but firm pressure.

If plants are grown in metal cans, have the cans cut to make removal easier. The rootball should be moist to avoid shattering.

After freeing any tangled or circled roots, position the plant in the hole slightly deeper than it was in the can. Backfill with reserved soil, remove any air pockets, and water immediately.

Stake tall or willowy plants with thin sticks or bamboo poles. Tie loosely with commercially available ties.

Remove any that are dry and brittle or appear to have rotted. Take as little time as possible to get them into the ground: it doesn't take long for wind and sun to dry out the tiny root hairs that are essential to life during the first few weeks after transplanting.

Before planting, take a good look at your plan to make sure you know what plants you want in which locations and how far apart they should be spaced. Some gardeners place tiny stakes to indicate locations.

Dig the holes large enough so that roots won't be cramped when you spread them out. The depth of the hole will be determined by the root system of the plant. Generally speaking, the point where the roots meet the stem or crown should be placed right at or slightly below ground level.

After you have inserted the plant, pack the soil around the root system gently. When the hole is filled you can firm it down with your feet to make sure there are no empty spaces between roots and soil. Water the plant thoroughly. This is also the best time to label the plants for future reference.

Transplanting Started Plants

If you ordered started plants from a mail-order source or purchased them in cell-packs or gallon cans from your garden center or nursery, the planting procedure is basically the same.

Small plants in cell-packs can be removed easily by pushing up on the bottom of the individual cell. Don't try to pull the plant out by the stem: it may not have an extensive root system and the top could break away from the roots. With a trowel, dig small holes roughly the same depth as the rootball. Take the plants out one by one and plant them *slightly* deeper than they were in the pack. Firm the soil around them and water thoroughly.

Larger perennials may be planted in plastic or tapered metal cans. Plants can be removed easily if the rootball is moist by turning the can over with your hand across the top and shaking it slightly or tapping the edge of the can on a table or a large rock. If the plants are in straight-sided metal cans and you plan on planting them right away, have the cans cut at the nursery. If you intend to hold the plants awhile before planting, leave the cans intact and cut them later yourself with a pair of tin snips. (Cut cans are almost impossible to water thoroughly.)

Be sure to loosen the circling roots around the rootball and spread them out before planting, so they won't girdle the plant. It's a good idea to loosen the rootball with a fork or your hands to make sure the roots spread out into the soil.

Staking

Staking is controversial among ardent perennial gardeners: some dislike the task so much that they refuse to plant any varieties that need it. There are two types of plants that require staking: those with tall single stalks, such as delphinium, hollyhock, and gladiolus; and those with many floppy stems, such as asters, chrysanthemums, coreopsis, heliopsis, and carnations.

As indicated in the illustration, tall, thin poles, such as the commonly available bamboo stakes, make the best supports for the single-stem plants. Simply place the stake an inch or so from the main stalk and shove it far enough into the ground to be stable. Attach the stalk to the stake with a plant tie, forming the tie into a figure eight as shown, so as not to cut into the stem but still allow some natural back-and-forth movement.

The favored method for staking lower, bushier plants is to use the twining prunings from fruit or ornamental trees, cut into lengths of about 16 to 20 inches. When the plants are about half that height, push the dried branches into the ground, placing several in a circular pattern around the clump. These provide a natural framework to support the plant and will become less noticeable as the plant grows.

An old-fashioned way to support a clump of tall-growing perennials is to place the previous year's twiggy prunings in the ground around the plants. As they grow they will be supported by the twigs and eventually hide them from view.

Fertilizing

Although not absolutely necessary, a midsummer feeding will benefit most plants. You can use the same product you used in conditioning your soil (preferably a dry fertilizer with a 5–10–5 or similar formulation), but apply it at a lower rate, about 2 pounds per 100 square feet. This will ensure that the plants are well fed and go into the winter as vigorous and healthy as possible.

If any individual plants in the garden seem to lag and need additional feeding during the growing season, you can mix a liquid fertilizer with water and apply it to those plants only. Most of the liquid formulations are fast-acting and it's easy to control the amount you apply, just the thing for "touch-up" feedings. It's best to make such feedings with half-strength or even weaker solutions: too little can be remedied; too much can't.

Liquid fertilizers are also valuable for *foliar feeding*, spraying the fertilizer mixture onto the leaves and stems of the plant. For perennials, early spring growth is usually limited by cold soil, even when the air is warm. Under such conditions soil microorganisms are not active to convert nutrients into a form the roots can absorb. But if the nutrients were available, the plant would grow. A nutrient spray on the foliage will provide immediate nourishment, allowing the plant to begin growth before the roots are able to absorb food from the soil.

Remember, though, that foliar feeding is a supplement to soil nutrition, not a substitute. Nutrients applied to foliage are absorbed and used by the plant quite rapidly; absorption begins within minutes after application, and with most nutrients is completed within 1 to 2 days.

Watering

The amount of water needed in the garden depends upon climate. Where summer rains are frequent you may need to irrigate only during an occasional dry spell; but in parts of the arid West and Southwest, watering is one of the gardener's biggest chores.

Whatever your climate, the simple rule for watering correctly is this: when you water, water well, and learn how long it takes the soil to dry out between waterings. The best way to tell if you've watered thoroughly is to take a trowel or shovel and check to see if the soil is moist 3 or 4 inches down. If it is, you know the water is reaching the root zone of the plants. This is absolutely necessary; superficial waterings are a waste and can actually harm plants by encouraging roots to grow toward the surface.

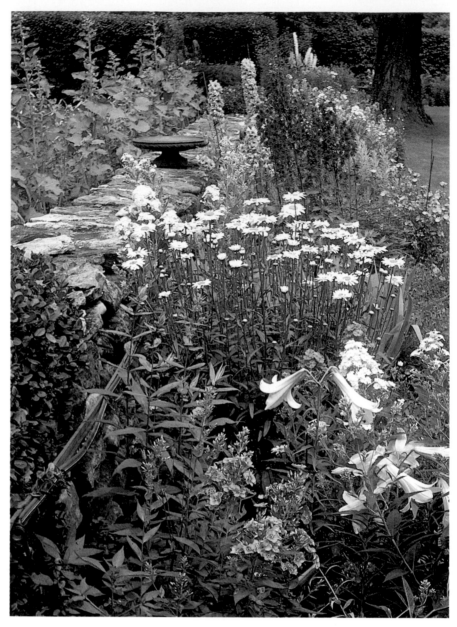

A time-saving, effective method of watering any flower bed or border is to use a soaker hose. Look carefully at the photograph and you'll find one. Soaker hoses can be installed as in this garden or just laid directly on the soil among the plants.

Watering a flower border or bed is best done with a canvas or plastic soaker hose laid more or less permanently among the plants. When you irrigate, turn the water on at a low level to keep the foliage as dry as possible. Try to water during the morning so that the garden can dry off a bit before nightfall: wet foliage will make the plants more susceptible to disease organisms. Of course, it is all right to spray plants occasionally with the hose or to use overhead sprinklers to remove dust and sediment from the air, if you're careful to do it early enough that plants can dry before evening.

Mulching

When spring is definitely in the air, the perennials are in the ground, the soil has warmed, and you have pulled any weeds that have appeared, apply 2 to 3 inches of mulch over the bed or border, tapering it off gradually as you get close to the plants. (A thick layer of moist mulch right next to a plant's stem can encourage pests and disease.)

Applying mulch in spring keeps the soil temperature cooler, which helps root growth; keeps the soil moisture at a more even level, thus reducing the amount of water needed; keeps a majority of summer weeds from establishing themselves; and aids in the long-term development of a good soil structure. These virtues add up to better growing conditions for the plants and a much easier job of maintenance for you.

Almost any organic material can serve as mulch, and the most highly recommended are: finely ground fir or pine bark, pine needles, compost, well-rotted manure, and, where available, redwood soil conditioner. Peat moss unfortunately makes a poor mulch because it forms a crust on top that is nearly impenetrable by water.

If you have a large quantity of leaves each fall and access to a shredder, you can make an excellent mulch and soil amendment. Just shred the leaves, stack the product in a pile, and leave it uncovered over the winter. By spring it will have decomposed. When the weather warms, turn the pile to let it dry out enough to apply easily.

In areas with extremely cold winters and a heavy snow cover, you'll want to protect your plants from the threat of *heaving*, the forcing out of the ground the plants can suffer as a result of alternate freezing and thawing. When the soil is thoroughly frozen to a depth of 2 inches, apply a layer of open, fluffy material such as pine boughs, excelsior, salt hay, or straw over the entire bed or border. This will keep the ground frozen until spring. Note that if you apply this protection any earlier, it may serve as a winter home for mice and other rodents still afoot, who may then feed on the roots and crowns of your plants through the season.

Pest and Disease Control

As a group, perennials are remarkably free of most pest and disease problems. With a daily stroll in the garden, you can hold potential problems to a minimum just by keeping your eyes open for anything irregular: a chewed leaf, a disfigured bud, stunted foliage, a small patch of mildew or rust on a leaf, and so on.

If you take action at the first sign of attack, less damage is likely, and you'll also minimize the need for chemical controls.

You can avoid problems by taking these steps:

☐ Keep old leaves picked up; they often harbor disease organisms and are safe hiding places for snails, slugs and many damaging insects.

☐ Pull weeds early, before they can compete with surrounding plants and

Any gardener with a little experience can tell you about the benefits of applying an organic mulch in spring. Mulches not only cut down on weeding and watering chores, but can be attractive as well.

produce seeds for more weeds. The best time to weed is when the ground is soft from rain or watering.

☐ Remove and destroy any diseased leaves, flowers, or fruits. Do not put them on the compost pile. Disease spores can live from one season to the next.

☐ Practice a thorough cleanup before winter sets in. Remove any debris and other likely homes for overwintering insects and diseases.

If a pest or disease does become a problem in your garden, consult the chart on pages 54–55 for the best controls. The more common problems are listed in the chart. More specific pests and diseases are discussed for individual plants in the Plant Selection Guide.

Dividing

There are basically three reasons for dividing perennials: control of size, rejuvenation, and propagation.

The nature of most perennials is to grow larger every year, usually by spreading and making a larger clump. Left alone, the most vigorous growers can expand until they choke out many desirable plants. As the clumps expand, they begin to compete with themselves; those plants on the outer edge thrive in fresh soil, but those in the center suffer from competing for moisture, nutrients, light, and air. You can end up with a healthy circle of plants around a dying center, not an attractive sight.

Except in areas of the country with extremely cold winters (temperatures

Aphids

Soft-bodied, green, brown, or reddish insects that suck plant juices. *Symptoms:* clusters of insects on shoots, flower buds or underside of leaves. Foliage and blooms stunted or deformed. Sticky honeydew attracts ants. *Solutions:* Lady beetles feed on aphids. Wipe out infestations with contact sprays such as Diazinon, Malathion, Sevin, or ORTHENE.

Beetles

Beetle larvae eat plant roots. *Symptoms:* Foliage, flowers, and stems are chewed, devoured, or have holes drilled in them. *Solutions:* Pick off beetles by hand or knock them into a can of kerosene and water. Spray with Diazinon, Malathion, or Sevin.

Botrytis Blight

(Gray Mold) A fungus disease that overwinters on infected plant parts. It attacks weak and dying foliage, flowers, and especially old, dying flowers. *Symptoms:* Grayish-brown growth on buds and flowers often appears fuzzy. The diseased flowers come apart easily when touched. *Solutions:* Pick off and destroy faded and infected blooms. Spray with fungicides. Read labels for recommendations.

Caterpillars

Larvae of moths and butterflies that feed on foliage, buds, and flowers. *Symptoms:* flower buds eaten or leaves rolled and tied around the pest and eaten from inside. Most often a problem in spring. *Solutions:* Cut out invested buds and leaves. Apply Diazinon or Sevin.

Damping Off

A fungus disease that is most often a problem in damp soil. *Symptoms:* Stems of young seedlings rot at ground level and fall over. Seedlings may also fail to emerge (preemergent damping off). *Solutions:* Do not overwater seedlings. Treat seeds with Captan, Phygon, Spergon, or Thiram.

of −10° to −20°F.), fall is the best time to divide perennials. The general rule is to divide spring- and summer-blooming perennials in late summer or fall, and to divide fall-blooming perennials in early spring, to give them a whole growing season to re-establish themselves. If you live in a climate with extreme winters, it's best to divide in early spring rather than subject newly planted divisions to the rigors of the weather.

Before dividing, decide what plants you want to save, which you want to dig out altogether, and which you want to replant elsewhere. To make digging and dividing easier, water the bed well a few days beforehand. So that you can see what you are doing, first prune the perennials severely, to 6 inches from the ground.

The actual dividing process is simple. Dig the entire clump out as completely as possible. If the center of the clump has died out, divide the living portion into smaller clumps to replant where you like. Where roots are so ensnarled that you can't simply pull the plants apart, you can cut them apart, but this is likely to do severe root damage. The best way to divide a stubborn clump is to insert two spading forks into it back-to-back, then press the handles toward each other, using the leverage at the tines to pry the clump apart.

The hole from which the clump was taken should be enriched with some organic matter and a handful of 0–10–10 fertilizer (or some similar formulation with no nitrogen). You can replace one or more of the divisions in the hole and replant the rest elsewhere or give them away to gardening friends.

If a clump of perennials proves hard to divide, insert two spading forks back-to-back and press the handles together, using just enough pressure to separate the roots.

Fungus Diseases

(Including powdery mildew and rust). Spread by wind and splashing water and overwinter on plant debris. *Symptoms:* Powdery mildew is shown by white powdery masses of spores on leaves, shoots, and buds; distorted shoots; or stunted foliage. Rust is shown by yellow dots and light green mottling on upper leaf surface opposite pustules of powdery, rust-colored spores on the lower surface. *Solutions:* For powdery mildew, apply Dinocap or PHALTAN. For rust, apply fungicides as recommended on labels. For both, remove and destroy all infected plant parts and debris.

Mites

Minute pests that suck juices from underside of foliage. *Symptoms:* Stippled leaves appear dry; turn brown, red, yellow, or gray; then curl and drop off. Webs may be visible on the underside of leaves. *Solutions:* Clean up trash and weeds in early spring to destroy breeding places. Spray with Kelthane.

Thrips

Tiny, brownish-yellow, winged insects. *Symptoms:* flecked or silver-white streaking and stippling on foliage and flowers. *Solutions:* Cut off and dispose of spent blooms. Apply Diazinon, Malathion, ORTHENE, or Sevin.

Virus Diseases

(Including Mosaic and Aster Yellows) Spread by propagation of infected plants, aphids, and sometimes leafhoppers. *Symptoms:* mottling or mosaic patterns on leaves; stunted or distorted growth. *Solutions:* Dispose of entire affected plants. Prevention is the best control.

White Flies

Nymphs are scalelike, flat, oval, pale green, brown, or black, depending on the species. *Symptoms:* Pure white adults are easy to see. Leaves become mottled, may turn yellow and die. *Solutions:* Spray with Diazinon, Malathion, or ORTHENE.

THE ART OF PERENNIAL GARDENING

Perennial gardening as an art form reached its peak in the nineteenth and early twentieth centuries. A look at some outstanding gardens will give you ideas you can apply to your own garden.

There is a unique dimension to gardening with perennials that for many gardeners greatly increases the pleasure of growing them: they are plants with a rich heritage, one that dates back through recorded history, and which attained rare heights in 19th-century England, when perennial gardening was widely practiced and refined into an art.

For many generations of English gardeners, perennials have been the backbone of the typical home garden. There had been no particular style or design associated with these gardens, just a love on the part of the gardener for the easily grown plants and their beautiful flowers. Later, these gardens would be termed "cottage gardens" (see page 12).

The familiarity and ease of culture of perennials led to some contempt for them during the Victorian era, when the demand for exotic plants rose to a peak. During this period, perennials were relegated to the backstage, considered by many as coarse "country cousins" to the more fashionable annuals that had been introduced into England and America from distant lands.

It became the popular form of gardening among the wealthy Victorians to surround one's mansion with lavish displays of tender annuals in severely geometric patterns. Huge formal beds were imposed upon the landscape almost like artists' canvases and made ready for temporary displays of color. With no regard for their individuality, annuals were mass-planted in elaborate configurations designed primarily to be seen from an elevated viewing position. Today, you can see similar displays in public parks and municipal gardens, where annuals are frequently used in large beds to spell out words or to create specific designs. (It is also interesting to note that the term "bedding plants" originally referred only to annuals, and that annuals were used almost exclusively in bed plantings.)

Because many of these plants had originally come from countries with warm climates, they had to be coaxed into bloom in England in coal-heated greenhouses. It wasn't unusual for one display to be planted out, soon to be replaced with an entirely new one lest the owner and guests become bored by the same display. Obviously, this type of gardening demanded a great deal of time and money and a large staff of gardeners. As novel and exotic as the new plants were, their cultural requirements, as well as the prevailing style of planting them, put them beyond the reach of most gardeners.

The Return of Perennials

England has long been a nation of ardent gardeners, and it seems that each generation has had its own gardening "voice." In the late 19th century that voice belonged to William Robinson (1838–1935). Robinson not only pointed out the wastefulness of composing formal gardens of tender annuals, but labeled these gardens unnatural and unattractive as well. His was an attitude whose time had come.

Robinson favored "wild" or "natural" gardens, where special qualities of each plant could be highlighted. He was adamantly against using plants to further the geometry or architectural features of a garden. He declared that, for all intents and purposes, the flowering plants in the Victorian annual beds might just as well have been colored bricks or stone. Robinson regularly put forth these somewhat strident views in his popular gardening magazine, *The Garden*.

In 1875 Robinson met Gertrude Jekyll (1843–1932), and because they shared similar viewpoints on gardening, Jekyll started contributing to the magazine.

Gertrude Jekyll began her career as an artist, but when her eyesight began to fail, she turned her artistic talents to gardening and writing about gardening. Although a woman of means, she was more influenced by the small, jumbled cottage gardens she observed in the countryside than by the great formal estate gardens. Scholars agree that it was Robinson who planted the seed of discontent regarding formal gardens, but it was Jekyll who brought the seed to flower in a popular form of gardening known as the "perennial border."

The cottage gardens that Jekyll admired must have impressed her as both a gardener and an artist. Although they lacked sophistication and grand

"The first purpose of a garden is to give happiness and repose of mind, which is more often enjoyed in the contemplation of the homely border..., than in any of those great gardens where the flowers lose their identity, and with it their hold of the human heart, and have to take a lower rank as mere masses of color filling so many square yards of space."
—Gertrude Jekyll

Right: An American garden shows the distinct influence of the Jekyll-Lutyens tradition. Rustic architecture and the casual cottage-style garden are a timeless combination.

scale, these small gardens had a quality that the most monumental Victorian gardens lacked; namely, a respect for the plants themselves and a randomness in the way they were planted, a randomness more commonly associated with plants in the wild.

The rekindling of interest in perennial gardens would have stopped there if Jekyll had not been an artist. She took what she liked best about the cottage gardens, saw how they could be improved and made more beautiful, and refined her ideas. As a painter, she had an intuitive respect for color. To her, the perennial border represented the opportunity to create beautiful, living paintings.

A young English architect named Edwin Lutyens (1869–1944) met Jekyll early in his career, and the two formed a long-lasting and important partnership.

Lutyens designed houses that were also a reaction against the formality and artifice of the Victorian period. Often built of native materials (stone, shingles, thatch, and the like), they had, regardless of their size, the cozy appearance of a cottage or farmhouse. He was a master at using stone, particularly for walls, paths, and garden pools. This stonework provided a strong architectural framework for the garden, but when combined with Jekyll's sensitive and seemingly random plantings, the effect was anything but formal.

The partnership of Lutyens and Jekyll was a popular one, both in England and on the continent. Together they were commissioned to do many houses and gardens, some still in existence, and their continuing influence testifies to their skill and artistry.

The gardens Jekyll designed and wrote about were composed of plants chosen for their individual foliage and flower qualities, with a sharp eye for how each related to the scene as a whole. Although many of Jekyll's gardens were large, they were always planned on the human scale. They were filled primarily with perennials, but annuals, bulbs, shrubs, vines, and herbs—often in surprising combinations—also had their places.

Gardeners today may think of the classic perennial border as a rather formal style of gardening, but in England in the 19th and early 20th century, the popularization of perennials was a welcome relief from the formality and rigidity of gardening with annuals. The movement away from tender annuals was significant in two ways: it shifted the plants from free-standing beds or islands to the more practical garden border; and it was composed of plants climatically adapted to the region. The hardy perennial border was something any gardener, regardless of wealth or gardening space, could achieve and have success with.

Two famous gardens, still very much alive and flourishing, embody the spirit of Jekyll's teachings. One is Vita Sackville-West's garden at Sissinghurst Castle in Kent, England; the other the garden surrounding the home of the impressionist painter Claude Monet in Giverny, France. Both gardens are open to the public today.

Sissinghurst

Vita Sackville-West (1892–1962) and her husband, Sir Harold Nicolson, bought Sissinghurst Castle in 1930. Together they planned the gardens there, but it is her contribution that is best remembered because in addition to being a fine gardener, she was also a prolific writer. From 1947 to 1961 she wrote a popular weekly garden column for the *Observer*. These columns were gathered together at various times and published in book form. Several of these books are still available.

In the foreword of one collection titled *V. Sackville-West's Garden Book*, Phillipa Nicolson states that over the years Sackville-West never stopped experimenting, but gradually developed several ironclad principles of gardening:

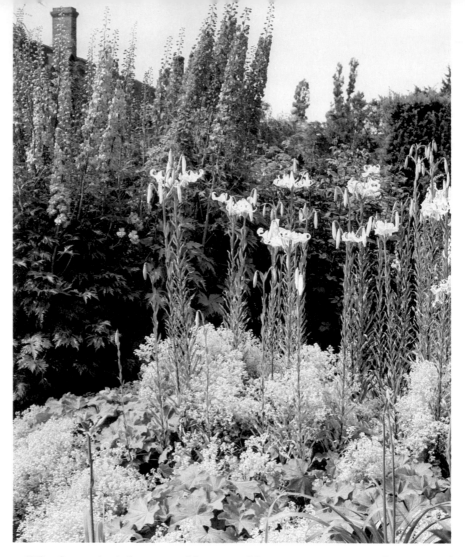

One of Vita Sackville-West's gardens at Sissinghurst Castle, England. Spires of deep lavender delphiniums tower above white *Lilium testaceum* and the lower-growing chartreuse *Alchemilla mollis*.

"Gardening is largely a question of mixing one sort of plant with another sort of plant, and of seeing how they marry happily together; and if you see that they don't marry happily, then you must hoick one of them. . . . That is the only way to garden."
—Vita Sackville-West

"The first principle was ruthlessness. You must never retain for a second year what displeased you in the first. It must be eradicated. Secondly, she was the opponent of too much tidiness. Let self-seeded plants grow where they naturally fell; let wild flowers sometimes be allowed to invade the garden; if roses stray over a path, the visitor must duck. But thirdly, there must be a plan—an architectural plan and a colour plan and a seasonal plan."

One of the most memorable and impressive of the individual gardens at Sissinghurst is the all-white garden. This garden has been the inspiration for many other similar gardens in all parts of the world. The principles on which it is based originated with Gertrude Jekyll's idea of a "tonal" garden, and when it was in its planning stages, Sackville-West wrote:

"For my own part, I am trying to make a grey, green, and white garden. This is an experiment which I ardently hope may be successful, though I doubt it. . . .

"My grey, green, and white garden will have the advantage of a high yew hedge behind it, a wall along one side, a strip of box edging along another side, and a path of old brick along the fourth side. It is, in fact, nothing more than a fairly large bed, which has now been divided into halves by a short path of grey flagstones terminating in a rough wood seat. When you sit on this seat, you will be turning your back to the yew hedge, and from there I hope you will survey a low sea of grey clumps of foliage, pierced here and there with tall white flowers. I visualize the white trumpets of dozens of Regale lilies, grown three years ago from seed, coming up through the grey of southernwood and artemisia and cotton-lavender, with grey-and-white edging plants such as *Dianthus* 'Mrs. Sinkins' and the silvery mats of

Stachys lanata, more familiar and so much nicer under its English names of Rabbits' Ears or Saviour's Flannel. There will be white pansies, white peonies, and white irises with their grey leaves . . . at least, I hope there will be all of these things. I don't want to boast in advance about my grey, green, and white garden. It may be a terrible failure. I wanted only to suggest that such experiments are worth trying, and that you can adapt them to your own taste and your own opportunities."

Her fears were unfounded. The white garden at Sissinghurst continues to bloom today, and each year visitors take away a vision of how beautiful a garden can be when it is planned and planted with a clear purpose in mind.

Monet's *Le Pressoir*

Claude Monet (1840–1926) is unquestionably one of the greatest and best-loved French impressionist painters. In 1883 he moved himself, his future wife, and their collective family of eight children to a rented house in Giverny (about 40 miles northwest of Paris) known as *Le Pressoir* (the cider press). Monet immediately started a garden "so that there would be flowers to paint on rainy days." But it wasn't until 9 years later, after he had purchased the house, that he began creating the garden which was to be immortalized in his paintings.

For the first few years, Monet and his crew of children planned and tended to the garden. By 1892 the garden had become so large that he hired a staff of six gardeners and built several greenhouses in which to start flowers. From Claire Joyes' excellent book, *Monet at Giverny*, comes this account of his gardening activity:

"Monet gave daily orders, inspecting the garden several times a day. No detail escaped him; he would correct a vista, recompose a clump of flowers, alter a pattern, and he insisted on the removal of fading blossoms. He planned his flower beds according to the principles that governed his palette, with light colours predominating and monochrome masses in juxtaposition. Very little soil was left bare in the garden; no flowers of

Vita Sackville-West's famous all-white garden at Sissinghurst continues to bloom today much as it did when she was alive. It is an exquisite garden that cannot help but impress the visitor. Among the plants are hydrangea, foxglove, candytuft, foamflower, lamb's ears, silver mound, delphiniums, and several old varieties of roses.

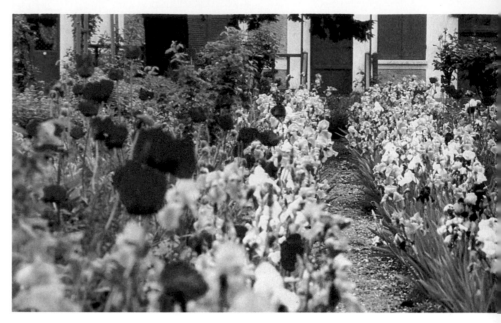

Monet's garden at Giverny, France, as it appears today, after the recent restoration. This part of the garden is a re-creation of a scene that appears in Monet's painting, "Garden at Giverny."

"My garden is slow work, pursued with love, and I do not deny that I am proud of it. Forty years ago, when I established myself here, there was nothing but a farmhouse and a poor orchard. I bought the house and little by little I enlarged and organized it ... I dug, planted, weeded, myself; in the evenings the children watered." In 1924, two years before his death, Monet said: "I perhaps owe having become a painter to flowers."
—Claude Monet

a fancy variety, no coloured or variegated foliage were allowed, and he was particularly fond of briar roses and of star-shaped dahlias with tubular petals.

"Although the layout of the flowerbed had a geometric basis, there was none of the formality of the typical French garden. Rectangles and straight lines disappeared under the spreading mats of nasturtium, wild geranium, aubretia and pink saxifrage. It was a painter's garden, where everything followed a certain rhythm, the supple tall stems of iris, lilies, foxgloves alternating with wild plumes of grasses and the bold masses of poppies and eschscholzias; where harmonies of tawny yellow, crimson and gold, saffron and blue were contrasted. Every item in the garden was designed to play a part; even the straight furrows in the raked garden paths were not a chance effect."

Monet died in 1926, leaving the house and garden to his son, Michel Monet. The son did not care in any special way for Giverny, and for over 50 years the estate was abandoned, during which time both the house and the garden fell into complete disrepair.

In 1966 Michel Monet died and willed the property to the *Institut de France*. After the *Institut* named Gerald Van der Kamp as the Conservator of the Claude Monet Foundation at Giverny, he faced the familiar and difficult task of finding the funds for the restoration process. The task was helped considerably by an early contribution of over one million dollars from an American benefactress, Lila Acheson Wallace.

After several years of painstaking work, the house and garden at Giverny was opened to the public for the first time in the summer of 1980. Today the gardens bloom again, and the house looks exactly as it did when Claude Monet lived, gardened, and painted there. From all accounts, a visit to Giverny is one well worth making.

Garden Restoration

For one reason or another, more and more people are buying older homes, with the intention of authentically restoring them in the way that corresponds to their particular period in architectural history. Large and small Victorian homes, rustic Craftsman bungalows, colonial farmhouses, and brownstone rowhouses frequently receive massive investments of effort and energy from new owners. Once the restoration work is completed, though, the gardens often need the same care and eye for detail that went into work on the house, in order to complete the picture. In almost all cases, unique period architecture had an equally unique style of gardening associated with it.

If you are interested in restoring or creating a garden to fit a period house, you may be frustrated in trying to locate information on what the garden might have looked like in the past, and what types of plants might have been grown there. Local libraries, historical societies, and title companies often maintain large collections of photographs taken in much earlier times. You may not find a picture of your own house as it looked way back when, but you will begin to get a feeling for what the gardens were like during the period by carefully scrutinizing these old photographs. And don't overlook the opportunity to talk with elderly neighbors; they may have vivid recollections of what the surrounding gardens once looked like.

Although there are few books available today that deal solely with period gardens, there are many books that deal with specific architectural styles. Many of these offer chapters relating to gardens and appropriate landscape styles. Even if no landscape information is given, photographs in architecture books can often give you ideas for creating a garden that is in keeping with the style of your house.

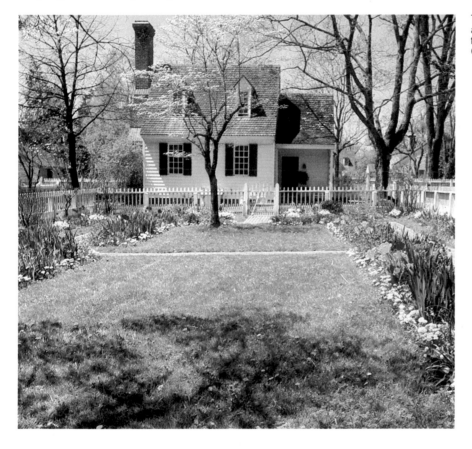

The creation of an appropriate garden to accompany a restored home can complete the picture of the period. This is a restored Colonial garden at Williamsburg, Virginia.

PLANT SELECTION GUIDE

The characteristics of more than a hundred favorite perennials are given here to help you choose the most suitable plants for your climate, soil, needs, and enjoyment.

There are literally thousands of perennials from which to choose, including an enormous number of cultivars and varieties. How, then, do you pick the best ones for your garden?

The selection process can begin here. While this guide by no means presents all of the available perennials, the species and varieties here are the most dependable, the most widely available, and the most adaptable to a wide range of climate and cultural conditions. Also included are some others that fit special conditions or special uses in the garden or landscape.

In choosing perennials for your own garden, you may find it best to first skim through the guide, noting the plants that catch your eye and jotting them down on a piece of paper. If you are looking for plants to meet specific needs, the lists on pages 35–41 will help you locate them quickly. The chart on page 27 will show you when they flower and what combinations and sequences of bloom are possible.

The next step is to read about the plants in more detail, keeping in mind these three questions.

☐ Will this plant work? This is a question of function, whether the plant fills the intended role. Color, size, shape, texture, and flowering date should all be considered.

☐ Will it grow in my garden? Many complex and varying factors enter into this question; but if the plant is hardy in your region, and if the requirements of soil, moisture, and light described fit your conditions, then the chances of success are excellent.

☐ Will this plant please me? This question addresses the personal tastes of the gardener. While seemingly an obvious one, it is surprising how often this all-important criterion is overlooked in the rush of sorting through the maze of cultural instructions and opinions of others. It does little good to choose a plant because it fits and thrives in your garden, if you don't like it.

To give you as complete a picture as possible of each plant, the guide includes detailed information on physical characteristics and cultural requirements. Some of this information is of necessity generalized, and may need to be adjusted for your area. For example, flowering dates and the best times for planting and dividing do vary regionally. In this guide these times apply to USDA Climate Zone 6, which, as you can see on the map on page 66, extends roughly on a line from Boston through Kansas City and into the Southwest. This "median" climate will serve as a general guide to give you some idea when to expect flowers, and when to plant and divide.

Flowering dates not only vary sometimes among climate zones, but can even vary from year to year in the same garden, by days or even weeks, depending on such factors as weather and horticultural practices. Planting and dividing in fall may be recommended for some areas, and in spring for the same plant in a different area.

No one book can possibly tell you how plants perform in all of the diverse

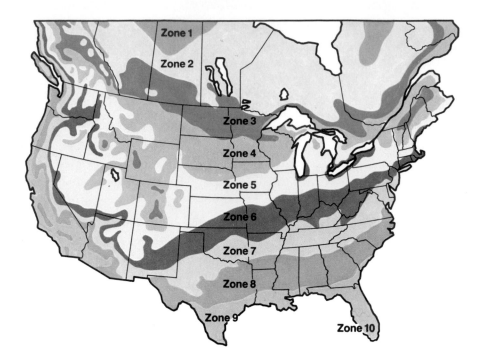

Climate Zones of the United States

Use this zone map to find your climate zone. Remember that these zones are approximate, based on average data, and that your local climate can be warmer or colder, especially in mountain regions. This map is based on the USDA map of climate zones.

Approximate Range of Average Annual Minimum Temperature for Each Zone

	Zone	Temperature
	Zone 1	Below −50°F
	Zone 2	−50° to −40°
	Zone 3	−40° to −30°
	Zone 4	−30° to −20°
	Zone 5	−20° to −10°
	Zone 6	−10° to 0°
	Zone 7	0° to 10°
	Zone 8	10° to 20°
	Zone 9	20° to 30°
	Zone 10	30° to 40°

Acanthus mollis 'Latifolius'

climatic conditions throughout the country; for this reason you should certainly double-check how the choices you make from this plant guide will perform in your specific area and climate. You can obtain this information from such sources as nurseries, agricultural extension agents, universities, botanic gardens, garden clubs, and gardening neighbors.

Beyond serving as a handy reference and a means of introducing and familiarizing yourself with the perennials, this guide may serve as inspiration and as a springboard for your own further explorations into the vast and intriguing world of perennial gardening.

Acanthus mollis (Bear's Breech). Acanthus family. Native to the Mediterranean region.

Bear's breech is grown for its clumps of immense, coarse, glossy leaves and tall flower spikes. It is usually considered more a landscape plant than a border perennial.

The dark green, deeply lobed leaves grow to 2 feet long, in basal clusters often 2 feet high and 4 feet wide. The foliage is imposing and effective from March to October.

The flowers are creamy white, lavender, or rose, with greenish or purplish bracts, and appear along upright stems 2 to 3 feet tall. They bloom in late spring and early summer.

How to Start: Best planted from divisions or nursery plants in spring.

Where to Plant: Best in moist, rich loam with good drainage, but it performs reasonably well in dry, sandy soil. It prefers filtered shade but tolerates full sun in cool climates. It tolerates drought, but foliage will be more lush with adequate moisture. In the northern limits of its range, plant in a warm, protected location, and mulch over winter. Space plants 3 to 4 feet apart. Bear's breech is a tender perennial, hardy in zones 8 through 10.

Care: Easy. Remove spent flower stalks. To grow for foliage alone, remove flower stalks as they appear. The roots spread a considerable distance underground, and the plant forms spreading clumps, like bamboo; so confine the roots unless you want a large stand. Snails and slugs can be a problem. The plant rarely requires division for rejuvenation, but is easily propagated by that method. Divide any time from October to March.

Varieties: *Acanthus mollis* 'Latifolius' has larger leaves and is hardier. It should be the choice for borderline areas in northern zone 8.

   A. mollis 'Oak Leaf' has larger leaves that are more deeply cut.

Achillea filipendulina (Fernleaf Yarrow). Daisy family. Native to Asia Minor and the Caucasus.

The fernleaf yarrow is an easy perennial with ferny, soft-textured foliage and large clusters of tiny yellow flowers. Some excellent related species and varieties have white or rose flowers.

   The flower clusters are flat on top and are held on elongated stalks. Flowering peaks from late June to mid-July, and the season can be prolonged by removing spent blossoms.

   The grayish foliage is dense almost to the ground and is effective all season. Growing 3 to 4 feet high, the plant is somewhat open and erect; but groups of three or more present a bushy appearance.

   The plant is long-lived and does not spread inordinately. It occasionally self-sows, but the seedlings will produce inferior plants.

How to Start: Divisions or nursery plants can be planted in early spring or fall. Named varieties may not come true from seed. Germinate indoors in February or March at 65° to 70°, and seeds will sprout in 5–7 days. Sow outdoors in early spring; seedlings will appear in 10–15 days.

Where to Plant: Soil must be well drained, preferably dry, and of only average fertility: too rich soil promotes weak growth and few flowers. Give it full sun. Yarrow tolerates drought and poor, dry soil. Place it away from wind to reduce the need for staking. The plant is hardy in all zones.

Care: Easy. Water only moderately and avoid excessive nitrogen fertilizer. Powdery mildew and stem rot are occasional problems, especially in moist climates. Avoid watering late in the day. The plant requires division every 3 or 4 years for rejuvenation. It propagates easily from divisions, which should be taken in early fall or spring.

Related Species and Varieties: *Achillea filipendulina* 'Coronation Gold' is lower growing, to 2 or 3 feet high, blooms most prolifically, and requires less staking.

   'Gold Plate' has huge flower clusters, up to 6 inches across, on tall, densely foliaged 4- to 5-foot plants.

   'Parkers Variety' has an open structure to 3½ feet high.

   'Moonshine' is low growing, to only 1½ feet tall, with silvery foliage and pale canary yellow flowers.

   A. millefolium 'Fire King' is also only 1½ feet tall, with flowers that open whitish and change to a deep rosy red. Flower clusters are 2 to 3 inches across and leaves are more finely textured than other yarrows.

   A. ptarmica 'Angels Breath' is 1 to 2 feet tall and produces great masses of

Achillea millefolium 'Fire King'

tiny double white flowers. It can be extremely invasive, especially in moist, rich soil. Divide at least every other year to restrain its growth; this may even need to be done annually.

Aconitum napellus (Aconitum Monkshood). Buttercup family. Native to northern Europe.

Caution: All parts of this plant are extremely poisonous; it should not be planted around vegetable gardens or where children play.

Monkshoods are tall, very hardy perennials that have excellent, glossy foliage and spikes of bluish flowers in August and early September. They are most useful in the rear of the border, and as a cut flower.

The flowers are intensely blue or violet blue, some bicolored with pale lavender, and some entirely lavender. They are oddly shaped, somewhat like a helmet or hood with a beak, and are produced in loose spikes atop 3- to 4-foot stems.

The dark green, glossy, deeply divided leaves present a medium-fine texture; and the foliage is effective from July until frost.

Monkshood, like delphinium, creates a strong vertical effect in the garden. Clusters of upright spikes are densely covered with leaves, especially toward the base. It is long-lived and quite restrained in growth.

How to Start: Planting divisions or nursery plants in autumn or early spring is best. Seed germinates slowly and erratically. Sow only fresh seed outdoors in fall.

Where to Plant: Native to thin woods and meadows in mountainous areas, monkshood prefers cool, moist but very well-drained soil rich in organic matter. Give it full sun or partial shade. The latter probably is best in hot climates. A location sheltered from heavy wind is best, but refrain from planting it near aggressive tree or shrub roots, as it does not compete well. Space plants 2 feet apart. Hardy to zone 3.

Care: Moderately easy. Water adequately, especially during drought or if in a hot location. Fertilize monthly during the growth period. Plants probably will require staking. Despite a long list of potential problems (crown rot, powdery mildew, aphids, mites, and several insect-borne virus diseases), aconite usually requires little protection. Avoid wet soil and don't let water remain on the foliage for any length of time. Practice good garden sanitation. If mites or aphids become a problem, apply pesticide regularly.

Division is easy and should be done in early spring or autumn. But the plant rarely requires division for rejuvenation or overcrowding, and often can go for many years without being disturbed.

Alchemilla vulgaris (Lady's Mantle). Rose family. Native to Europe.

Delicate, fluffy flowers arch from the refined grayish-green leaves of this plant, which is useful in the front of the border or as a ground cover in partial shade.

The flowers are chartreuse or yellowish green in color, and the plants bloom in June through August. They appear on curving stalks up to 18 inches long.

The leaves are 3 to 4 inches wide and rounded, with lobes creased like a fan. Slightly hairy, they catch droplets of water that sparkle in the sunlight. The foliage is effective all summer long.

Lady's mantle is long-lived and notoriously invasive, an advantage as a ground cover.

How to Start: Plant divisions or nursery bedding plants in early spring or autumn. Sow seed indoors in early spring at 65°, or sow directly outdoors. Seeds germinate in 8 days.

Where to Plant: The soil should be moist, well drained, and of average fertil-

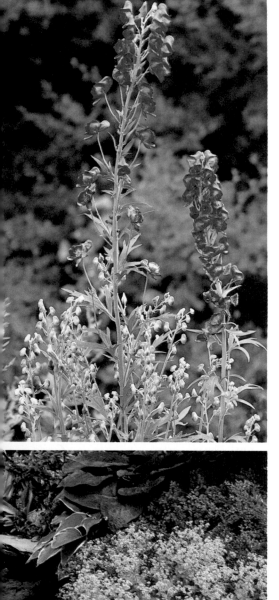

Below: *Aconitum* hybrid
Bottom: *Alchemilla vulgaris*

ity. The plant prefers partial shade, especially in hot climates. Space plants 10 inches apart and plant in clumps of three or more. Hardy to zone 3.

Care: Easy. Keep moist. Remove spent flowers to prevent rampant spreading. There are no serious pests. The plant can go for many years without requiring division for rejuvenation or thinning. To multiply, divide 3- or 4-year-old plants in autumn or early spring.

Amsonia tabernaemontana (Blue Star; Amsonia). Dogbane family. Native to the southeastern United States.

The blue star is refined and delicate, not the showiest perennial. Its clusters of small stars are effective for only 2 weeks in late May and early June (although in northern climates it has been known to bloom as late as July). The willowlike foliage, however, is attractive all summer long. The plant's chief advantages are that it is extremely easy to grow, restrained in growth, and care free.

The flowers are an unusual steel blue in color. Tiny and delicate, they appear in dense clusters at the ends of the stems.

The foliage is bright green all summer, turning brilliant gold in the fall. The leaves are long, narrow, and medium fine in texture. The clumps of multibranched stems are bushy and semi-erect, growing 2 to 3 feet tall and 1½ to 2 feet wide. The plant is very long-lived and grows slowly, never creating a spreading problem.

How to Start: Plant divisions or nursery plants in the fall. It can be grown from seed collected fresh and sown in fall. If sown in spring, first prechill for several weeks, then sow at 45°. Seeds sprout in 3 weeks.

Where to Plant: Blue star performs well in nearly any soil, moist or dry, but soggy soils should be avoided. It is best in partial shade, but tolerates full sun well. Space plants 12 to 15 inches apart. Hardy to zone 3.

Care: Extremely easy. The plant does best with regular watering and feeding. It has no serious pests. Division is never necessary, but it is an excellent way of propagating new plants. Divide in either spring or fall.

Anchusa azurea (Italian Bugloss; Italian Alkanet). Borage family. Native to the Mediterranean region.

Above: *Amsonia tabernaemontana*
Left: *Anchusa azurea*

Although the Italian bugloss is a short-lived plant, you can expect its clouds of pure, vivid blue flowers to remain in the garden for a long time; it is a prolific self-sower. Striking color is the only reason for growing this plant, as its foliage is coarse and unappealing.

The flowers appear in June and most of July. Individually they are tiny, but are borne profusely in large, loose clusters on the top third of the plant.

The foliage is dark green with bristly, hairy stems and leaves that become quite rangy and unattractive after blooming is completed. The plant is upright and spreading, with most foliage at the base. It grows 3 to 5 feet tall.

Anchusa self-sows prolifically and can become a nuisance. It is often treated as a fall-sown annual or biennial, and the flowers are best on 1- or 2-year old plants.

How to Start: Sow seed in late summer or early fall, or sow outdoors in the spring at 50° to 65°. Start indoors 6 to 8 weeks prior to the last frost in spring. Seedlings appear in 14 days.

Where to Plant: Anchusa performs well in nearly any soil, but is best in well-drained, moist loam of average to poor fertility. It prefers full sun but tolerates partial shade. The tallest varieties should be protected from wind. Plant 18 to 30 inches apart. Hardy to zone 3.

Care: Moderately easy. Water plentifully, especially during drought. Do not fertilize. Cut back after flowering to encourage a secondary (although usually inferior) bloom. Tall varieties will require staking. Crown rot in soggy soils is a serious problem.

Divide anchusa every year, or at least every other year. Thin self-sown seedlings to avoid crowding.

Varieties: 'Dropmore' grows 4 to 5 feet tall with huge clouds of bright blue flowers. It requires staking. 'Loddon Royalist' reaches only 3 feet in height. 'Pride of Dover' reaches 4 feet with lighter blue flowers, and requires staking. 'Royal Blue' has intense, deep blue flowers and grows to a compact 3 feet high.

Anemone × *hybrida* (Japanese Anemone). Buttercup family. Parents native to China, Japan, and Nepal.

The Japanese anemone displays attractive foliage and loose, open clusters of flowers in white and shades of pink. It is especially valuable for providing fall color in partial shade.

The flowers are each 1½ to 3 inches across, depending on variety and conditions of growth, and bloom in late summer to mid-autumn.

The leaves are dark to light green, large, deeply lobed, and pleasantly coarse in texture. Reminiscent of maple leaves, they are quite effective, especially during the flowering period. They cover the plant densely at the bottom and become smaller and sparser toward the top, leaving the upper 1 to 2 feet of stem bare. Japanese anemones grow 2 to 5 feet tall.

The plants slowly increase in size and number of flowering stems. They are well behaved, long-lived in favorable locations, and resent disturbance once established.

How to Start: Commercially produced rooted cuttings should be purchased in individual containers and planted in spring. To produce your own cuttings, place 2-inch pieces of roots in sandy loam outdoors in early spring, and keep evenly moist.

Where to Plant: Rich, moist soil high in humus. Soil must have good drainage; wet soil in winter is usually fatal. The plant prefers partial shade but tolerates full sun, especially in cool climates. Space plants 18 inches apart. Hardy to zone 6.

Care: Moderately easy. Water during dry spells in summer. In the northern

Anemone × *hybrida* with *Crocosmia* foliage in the foreground

limits of its hardiness range it is advisable to protect with a loose mulch, such as evergreen boughs. Do not apply this protection until the ground is frozen, however, or trapped moisture will kill it quickly. The black blister beetle can rapidly defoliate established plants.

Clumps rarely require division. If necessary, divide in early spring; success is usually difficult. For increase, root cuttings are better.

Anthemis tinctoria (Golden Marguerite). Daisy family. Native to Central and Southern Europe and Western Asia.

The golden marguerite produces masses of small golden yellow daisies on 2-foot bushy clumps in July. Although short-lived, it is useful in the border or for cut flowers.

The individual flowers are small, up to 2 inches in diameter, but are massed in profusion on long, strong stems. The plant blooms in July, but removing spent flowers before they set seed can prolong the season into September.

The fernlike leaves are dark green on the upper surface, white and woolly on the undersides. They are medium fine in texture, aromatic when bruised, and effective all season long. The foliage is dense and bushy, and grows 2½ to 3 feet tall. The plant self-sows prolifically, and can become a nuisance.

How to Start: Sow seed directly outdoors in spring or summer, or start indoors 6 to 8 weeks prior to setting seedlings out after the last frost in spring. Indoor germination will take from 1 to 3 weeks at 68° to 70°. Divisions or rooted cuttings can often be purchased; plant these in spring or early summer.

Where to Plant: Anthemis performs well in nearly any soil as long as it is well drained. Give it full sun. It tolerates hot, dry locations and poor soil remarkably well, but does not do at all well in heavy, wet, clay soils. Plant 15 to 18 inches apart. Hardy to zone 3.

Care: Moderately easy. Water only moderately. There are no serious pests. Anthemis must be divided every other year, at least, as clumps will die out in the center. Annual division may be required in moist climates. Divide in spring or fall.

Varieties: 'Moonlight' has pale yellow flowers; 'Beauty of Grallegh' has flowers of deep yellow; and 'E. C. Buxton' has very bright, yellow flowers.

Aquilegia species (Columbine). Buttercup family. Native to the cool northern temperate zones, mostly in North America and Europe.

Columbines are delicate, airy plants with curiously spurred, showy flowers in a wide range of colors and forms. They are useful in the border and in "wild" gardens.

The flowers come in shades of white, blue, purple, red, pink, yellow, orange, reddish brown, or nearly black, in solids or bicolors. They appear in May and June. Each bloom consists of five sepals and five tubular petals that extend into spurs beyond the rear of the blossom. Hybridizers have developed a huge array not only of color but of flower size from 1½ to 4 inches across and up to 6 inches long. The flowers nod gracefully at the ends of long, slender stems.

The foliage is light green, often with a slight silvery, dusty cast that catches and holds dewdrops. Notched, compound leaves give the plant an open, finely textured appearance somewhat like that of a maidenhair fern. Foliage can be effective into August if not attacked by leaf miners. The plant grows from 18 to 36 inches tall.

Columbine is usually short-lived, especially if the soil does not have perfect drainage. It does self-sow in favorable environments, but the offspring will differ, often radically, from hybrid parents.

Anthemis tinctoria

Aquilegia hybrid

How to Start: Plants can be started from seed, although young seedlings or divisions from a nursery are the usual methods. Sow seed outdoors in early spring or summer for flowers the next year. Or start indoors in a flat of sandy soil 12 to 14 weeks before setting out in mid-spring. Refrigerate the flat for 3 weeks, then put it in a moist, shady place at 70° to 75°. Do not cover the seeds, as indirect light is required for germination, which usually occurs in 3 to 4 weeks.

Where to Plant: These are predominantly woodland plants and as such prefer cool, moist soil rich in organic matter. Drainage must be excellent. They prefer filtered shade, but will tolerate full sun in cool-summer climates, although this will tend to shorten the flowering period. Space plants 12 to 24 inches apart. Hardy to zone 3.

Care: Moderately difficult unless species are grown. Water generously and give regular light feedings, applying fertilizer at half strength. The chief pests are the leaf miner and the columbine borer, which disfigure the foliage. Spray with malathion in early, middle, and late May, and carefully remove infected plants.

Division can be performed for increase in August and September; but it probably is best to keep new plants coming on by sowing fresh seed yearly. When dividing, break the clumps apart carefully and perform the operation quickly. Never allow the roots to dry out.

Armeria maritima (Sea Pink; Thrift). Leadwort family. Native to the coastal Mediterranean region.

The sea pink is a hardy evergreen perennial that forms dense cushions of grasslike foliage, from which small rounded flowers arise in colors of white or pale pink to deep rose. The plant is excellent for edging, rock gardens, cut flowers, and possibly for beds and borders.

The flowers appear in May and June, and sporadically the year round in mild climates. They are produced in dense, tiny heads about 1 inch in diameter, atop erect stems reaching 6 to 12 inches above the foliage.

The bright green, narrow leaves make a low, matlike mound 3 or 4 inches high; but size is quite variable from seed. The tufts of foliage gradually expand by short runners into clumps 1 to 1½ feet across. After about 4 years (sooner in overly moist locations) the center begins to die out, and division is necessary.

How to Start: Young plants are often purchased in flats or containers as divisions, but they are also easy to start from seed. Soak the seeds for several hours and then sow outdoors in spring or summer. Or start indoors, for setting out in early summer, by sowing in a flat of sandy soil and maintaining a temperature of 65° to 70°. Germination occurs in 2 to 3 weeks.

Where to Plant: Armeria must have excellent drainage, and will perform well in almost pure sand. It is best in dry, infertile soil and full sun. It tolerates constant wind and salt spray. Space plants 6 to 12 inches apart. Hardy to zone 3.

Care: Easy. Do not fertilize except in the poorest of soils, and then only lightly. Water only moderately. Excessive moisture and fertility hasten dying out in the center. Prolong flowering by judiciously removing faded flowers before they set seed. Do not mulch over winter or rot may result. The plant has no serious pests.

When the center of the clump begins to die, divide to rejuvenate. Division is an excellent means of propagation, and can be performed in spring, summer, or fall.

Related Species and Varieties: Armeria is quite variable from seed and many cultivars are listed. Where uniformity of size or color is desired, it is best to choose a named variety.

Armeria maritima

A. plantaginea is like a large *A. maritima*, growing 1½ to 2 feet tall. Although it is less frequently available commercially, its larger size makes it more suitable for a border. Like *A. maritima* it is extremely variable from seed. 'Bee's Ruby' has later, bright, deep red flowers in June and July.

Artemisia schmidtiana (Silver Mound; Wormwood; Angel's Hair). Daisy family. Native to Japan.

The silver mound is famous for its intense silvery gray, feathery foliage produced in neat, dense mounds. It is perhaps the most popular gray-foliage accent plant.

The leaves are heavily divided, have a very soft, fine texture, and form a bushy, rounded mound 12 inches high and 18 inches wide. The flowers are inconspicuous.

In perfect conditions the plant can be long-lived, but if the soil is over-moist, particularly during winter, it will not survive long. If soil is too rich, the foliage tends to become too lush and the plant will open at the center. It never spreads or reseeds.

How to Start: Stem cuttings are easy to root during the summer; most nursery plants are started this way. Set young plants out in spring.

Where to Plant: Silver mound must have perfect drainage; it will not tolerate soggy roots, especially in winter. Poor, dry, sandy soil and full sun are best. It tolerates heat, but is prone to rot in climates of excessive summer humidity. Space plants 18 to 24 inches apart. Hardy to zone 5.

Care: Easy. Avoid overwatering or fertilizing. Rust is the only serious pest, but fungicide is rarely required. Always water early in the day, and avoid letting water stand on the foliage for any length of time. Division is difficult, never necessary, and seldom successful.

Aruncus dioicus, formerly *A. sylvester* (Goatsbeard). Rose family. Native to Eurasia and North America.

Goatsbeard is a large, shrublike perennial that produces showy, silky white plumes in midsummer. The plant looks like a large astilbe and is excellent in partial shade in the rear of the border or as a shrub accent, particularly in combination with astilbe and filipendula.

Artemisia schmidtiana (Silver Mound) with *Astilbe*

Aruncus dioicus

Asclepias tuberosa

The flowers are minute and gathered into gracefully relaxed plumes that are often as long as 16 inches. They appear in mid-June to early July.

The foliage is medium green with large, compound leaves of bold texture. It lasts all season long. The plant is 5 to 7 feet tall, spreading 3 to 5 feet across. It is long-lived and, despite its large size, restrained in growth and not invasive.

How to Start: Seeds sown at 45° in early spring will germinate in 2 weeks. Set container-grown plants out in early spring.

Where to Plant: Moist, preferably rich soil high in organic matter. Aruncus is best grown in partial shade, such as under a high canopy of trees or on the east side of a building; but with sufficient moisture it tolerates full sun. Space plants 3 to 5 feet apart. Hardy to zone 4.

Care: Easy. Water generously and deeply. Fertilize regularly during the growing season. Despite its height, it never needs staking. It has no serious pests. The plant can go many years before needing division for rejuvenation. Division for increase is difficult and rarely successful.

Asclepias tuberosa (Butterfly Flower; Butterfly Weed). Milkweed family. Native from New England to North Dakota, south to Florida, Arizona, and New Mexico.

Brilliant orange-red clusters of flowers appear on this North American native in midsummer and attract hordes of butterflies, hummingbirds, and bees to the garden.

The flowers are most commonly found in deep orange; but cultivars from pale lemon to deep oxblood red are becoming available. The individual blooms are tiny, but appear in many dense clusters at the ends of the stems. They normally bloom from June to August, but peak from mid-June to early July. The milkweedlike fruits are attractive in dried arrangements.

The lance-shaped leaves are dark green and hairy. Each plant is composed of a cluster of stems, giving it an erect and slightly spreading form. It grows from 18 to 36 inches tall. The plant is restrained in growth and long-lived. Its deep tap root makes it drought tolerant but renders it difficult to divide or transplant.

How to Start: It is best to plant the tuberous bare roots when the plant is dormant in the fall or early spring. Set the bare tap root vertically into the soil so that the "eye" is 1 to 2 inches below the soil line. Seed-starting is possible, but germination is erratic and unpredictable. Sow seeds outdoors in May or indoors in early spring at 68° to 75°. Seedlings appear in 3 to 4 weeks.

Where to Plant: Native to meadows and prairies, asclepias is best in light, sandy, poor soil and full sun, but you can expect good performance in peaty soil or even heavy clay. Avoid excessively moist soils. It tolerates wind. Space plants 12 to 18 inches apart. Hardy to zone 3.

Care: Easy. Water only through drought, especially in heavy soils. It is slow to appear in the spring, so take care when cultivating around its area. There are no serious pests. Division is never necessary and is difficult and rarely successful.

Aster **species** (Hardy Aster; Michaelmas Daisy). Daisy family. The parents of many hybrids are native to North America, Europe, and Asia.

Familiar for their late-season color, asters produce daisylike flowers in late summer and fall, in all shades except orange. Many varieties are available in a wide range of flower colors and sizes. Although requiring frequent division, they are easy to grow.

The flowers are usually violet-purple or blue, but many shades of purple, red, pink, and white are also available. All have yellow centers. They are about 2 inches across and are produced in large clusters at the ends of the stems, blooming any time from August into October, depending upon variety.

The foliage is dark to dusty green and of medium-coarse texture. Leaves are hairy, sticky, and linear or lance-shaped. Low-growing varieties are bushy, prostrate, and spreading, creating dense carpets of color as low as 9 inches. Taller varieties range from 18 inches to 6 feet high, and their clusters of erect stems are heavily branched toward the top and densely covered with foliage.

The aster form is generally upright and spreading. Clumps increase quickly and begin to die out in the center at an early age, necessitating division. The plant reseeds sporadically, but the hybrids will not breed true to type. It is fairly short-lived without adequate maintenance.

How to Start: Named cultivars are best started by divisions, nursery plants, or hand-pollinated seed. Divisions of young plants are best set out in early spring. Sow seed outdoors in spring or early summer, or indoors in early spring. Sow thickly, as the percentage of germination is usually low. Seedlings appear in 2 to 3 weeks at 70° to 75°.

Aster hybrid

Where to Plant: Asters are not too particular about soil, but light, moist, well-drained soil of average fertility is best. They accept full sun or partial shade, preferring the latter in hot southern climates. Space plants 12 to 20 inches apart. Hardy to zone 4.

Care: Moderately easy to moderately difficult. The plant performs best with abundant water, but never allow roots to remain soggy. Feed only lightly. Pinch in late spring to produce better flowering and denser plants. Varieties over 2 feet tall will need support to protect them from wind and rain; the recommended method of staking is to provide twiggy branches through which the plants can grow up and around.

Rust and powdery mildew can be serious; so protect plants throughout the growing season with a weekly spraying of fungicide. Do not let moisture stand on foliage in cool weather or in the evening. Japanese beetles can also be a problem, particularly on earlier-blooming varieties. Later-blooming flowers usually open after the beetle season has run its course.

Division is necessary at least every other year, and often annually, as clumps start dying out in the center. Division is an excellent means of increase and should be done in early spring.

Related Species and Cultivars: *Aster × frikartii* 'Wonder of Stafa' is the best choice for the hot, humid summers of the Southeast. Its lavender-blue flowers, sometimes appearing as early as June, are effective well into October. It is marginally hardy in southern zone 6. Mulch well in the northern limits of its range to protect over winter. It grows 2½ feet tall and requires staking.

Astilbe **species** (False Spirea; Astilbe). Saxifrage family. Native to Eastern Asia.

Astilbe is a favorite perennial for shady, moist locations but also performs well in full sun. It offers glossy, dark green foliage and fluffy plumes of white, pink, lavender, or red flowers on erect or arching stems. The tiny flowers are produced in great quantities and the effect is delicate and feathery. It blooms in June and July.

The leaves are divided and compound. Sometimes tinged with bronze, they resemble a coarse fern and are always lush and refined. The foliage forms bushy mounds rarely exceeding 1 or 2 feet in height; the flowers often reach another 12 to 18 inches more. Most flower heads are erect and pyramidal; others arch gracefully.

Astilbe will gradually spread as clumps expand. Being a heavy feeder, it

Astilbe hybrid

will deplete the soil and flower less as years go by; but division every 3 or 4 years will rejuvenate the flowering. The plant is restrained in growth, not invasive, and long-lived.

How to Start: Divisions or nursery plants are best set out in spring. Nurseries frequently offer young container-grown plants. Seed is difficult to germinate and produces wide variability.

Where to Plant: A cool, moist location in light shade, with deep, rich soil high in organic matter. It does not tolerate wet winters well without adequate drainage, and will not take summer drought. It performs well in deep shade but accepts full sun if watered deeply and often. Space plants 1 to 2 feet apart. Hardy to zone 4.

Care: Moderately easy. Give generous applications of 5–10–10 fertilizer each spring just as growth begins. Water abundantly. Japanese beetles can be a serious pest. Powdery mildew, slugs, and snails also can be problems. Although the plant will perform adequately without division, for maximum flower size and quantity it is best to divide every 3 or 4 years. It is easy to propagate by dividing the root stock just as plants are beginning to grow in the spring.

Aurinia saxatilis

Aurinia saxatilis, formerly *Alyssum saxatile* (Basket-of-Gold; Golden-tuft). Mustard family. Native to Southern and Central Europe and Turkey.

Basket-of-gold is a low, bushy perennial of variable habit, covered with bright lemon yellow flowers in April and May. Useful in dry, poor soil, it is frequently grown in rock gardens.

Individually the flowers are tiny, but they are produced in incredible profusion, entirely covering the plant. The foliage is gray green, providing an interesting accent when the plant is not in bloom. The leaves are small, elongated, and cover the plant densely.

The form varies according to the selected cultivar and to growth conditions. In rich, moist soil it tends to be open and sprawling; in dry, poor soil it will be compact and bushy, 9 to 12 inches high and spreading to 12 or 15 inches. It is fairly short-lived.

How to Start: Plant divisions or nursery plants in early spring. Or sow seed outdoors in early spring. Seedlings appear in 1 to 2 weeks.

Where to Plant: Dry, poor, infertile soil in full sun is preferred, and drainage must be excellent. Plant 8 to 12 inches apart. Hardy to zone 3.

Care: Water only moderately through periods of drought. Do not fertilize. After blooming is over, cut the stems to half their length to keep the plant vigorous. It has no serious pests. Divide to increase in spring just as growth commences.

Baptisia australis (False Indigo). Pea family. Native to Pennsylvania, south to North Carolina and Tennessee.

False indigo is a large perennial with mildly showy spikes of flowers in late spring. Hardy, pest-free, and undemanding, this is one of the easiest perennials to grow. It is excellent for backgrounds and at the rear of the border, or as a shrublike mass in the landscape.

The flowers are often described as "indigo blue," but actually range from pale lavender to dark purple. They are pea-shaped, about 1 inch long, and are produced in long, erect spikes at the top of the branches, appearing in late May to early June.

The foliage is dense, lush, and remains attractive until hard frost in the fall. The cloverlike leaves are a clean, bright green, and divided into three leaflets.

False indigo forms shrubby, rounded masses 3 or 4 feet tall, sometimes taller, and equally as wide. It is restrained in growth, will not spread, and is long-lived.

Baptisia australis

How to Start: Best from young nursery plants. It is easy to grow from seed sown outdoors in late fall or early spring, but it will not begin to flower for 2 or 3 years. Propagating from division is difficult.

Where to Plant: Best in well-drained garden loam of average fertility. It tolerates nearly any soil except a very wet one. Give it full sun or partial shade, although there will be less flowering in shade. Plant 18 to 24 inches apart. Hardy to zone 3.

Care: Extremely easy. The tallest plants may require staking to prevent damage by high winds. Remove spent flowers to prolong bloom. (However, the black, long-lasting seed pods are considered attractive by many.) As a legume, it "fixes" its own nitrogen from the atmosphere, and needs little if any feeding. It prefers poor soil. Water only moderately.

Although powdery mildew and rust are reported, they are seldom serious problems. Due to the deep tap root, division is extremely difficult and seldom successful. Luckily, it is not necessary either for rejuvenation or propagation.

Belamcanda chinensis

Belamcanda chinensis (Blackberry Lily; Leopard Flower). Iris family. Native to China and Japan.

The blackberry lily produces great quantities of star-shaped flowers in late July and August. Orange with red dots, they measure about 2 inches across and appear on multibranched stems that can reach as high as 4 feet. The clusters of seeds that follow look like blackberries, and are attractive in dried arrangements.

The swordlike leaves are bright green to gray green and resemble those of tall bearded iris. They form large clumps of foliage 2 to 3 feet high.

Blackberry lily may reseed, but the seedlings are easy to weed out. The clumps expand slowly and the plant is long-lived.

How to Start: Easy to start from seed but faster from nursery plants or tubers divided and planted in the spring.

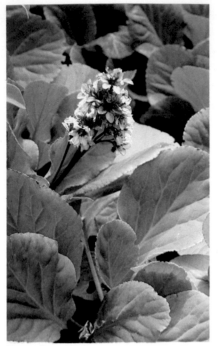

Bergenia cordifolia

Where to Plant: Belamcanda must have well-drained soil, as winter sogginess is usually fatal. Give it full sun. Space plants 1 to 3 feet apart. The plant is best used, however, as a single specimen. Hardy to zone 5.

Care: Easy in well-drained soil. In northern areas it should have a protective layer of loose mulch over winter. Iris borer can be a severe pest. See *Iris* (Bearded Iris) for recommendations. While division is an excellent means of propagation, clumps can go for many years without needing it for rejuvenation. Division is best performed in the spring or early fall.

Related Species: *Belamcanda flabellata* is similar in all respects except that the flowers are clear yellow and bloom slightly later, into September. It is less commonly available.

Bergenia cordifolia (Bergenia; Heart-Leaf Bergenia). Saxifrage family. Native to Siberia and Mongolia.

Bergenia is a low-growing evergreen perennial with large, rounded, cabbagelike leaves and pink or white flowers. Undemanding, adaptable to nearly any situation, and extremely hardy, it is useful in the front of the border or massed as a bed or ground cover.

The flowers are about ¾ inch wide and appear in clusters atop stems extending 6 to 12 inches above the foliage. They bloom in April and May normally, but may not appear at all in areas of severe winters or other harsh exposure.

The foliage is medium green in summer, with a reddish tinge in winter. Leaves are wavy-edged, fleshy, and measure 10 inches across, radiating in all directions from the base.

Measuring 12 to 15 inches high, the plant spreads by rhizomes that creep along the soil surface, to form dense mats of leaves. In excessively fertile situations it may leave bare spots as the clump expands. It grows slowly and could never be called invasive.

How to Start: While best started from divisions in early spring, it also can be raised from seed sown outdoors in late fall or early spring.

Where to Plant: Bergenia tolerates a wide variety of soils, performing well in poor, dry ones and rich, moist ones; but it prefers well-drained soil of average fertility. More frequent division is necessary in rich, moist soil. Give it either sun or shade. The latter is better in regions of hot summers. Space plants 12 to 18 inches apart. Hardy to zone 2.

Care: Easy. It responds vigorously to fertilizing, but this will also result in stretching, bare spots, and the need for more frequent division. Water only moderately for the same reason. It has no serious pests, but does provide a haven for snails. On dry sites with relatively infertile soil, it will not need division for years. In rich, moist soil it may need it about every 4 years.

Brunnera macrophylla (Siberian Bugloss). Borage family. Native to the Caucasus and western Siberia.

The tiny flowers of Siberian bugloss, produced in delicate clusters, resemble those of *Anchusa azurea*, the Italian bugloss. This plant, however, has the advantage of excellent, large, heart-shaped leaves that remain attractive all season long. In addition, it is easy and adaptable whether grown in full sun or shade.

The flower color is a clear sky blue, and blooms appear generously in branching, open clusters atop stems 12 to 15 inches tall. They bloom in April through May and somewhat resemble forget-me-nots.

The dark green leaves are clean, lush, and pest-free. They reach 6 to 8 inches long in July and grow in basal clumps about 12 inches high. The foliage is effective until frost.

Left: *Brunnera macrophylla*
Below: *Caltha palustris* 'Flore Pleno'

The plant expands outward gradually. It is well behaved, not invasive, and lives a long time without requiring division.

How to Start: By clump divisions taken in early spring, by nursery plants, or by seed sown outdoors in early fall. To sow seed in spring, freeze for 1 week to break dormancy; then sow in early spring at 45°. Germination takes 2 weeks.

Where to Plant: Exceedingly adaptable, the plant performs well in any soil, in sun or shade. Like most garden plants, however, it responds to a moist soil high in organic matter. Partial shade is best. Space plants 12 to 18 inches apart. Hardy to zone 3.

Care: Easy. It is best with abundant water and regular feeding, but does well with little attention. It has no serious pests. Division is needed if the center begins to die out, but this rarely occurs for many years.

Caltha palustris (Marsh Marigold). Buttercup family. Native to Eurasia and North America from Alaska to North Carolina.

The marsh marigold is a cheerful little plant for wet, soggy soil or standing water. It has bright golden yellow flowers about 1 inch across borne singly above the foliage. The bright green, rounded leaves are held horizontally on tall, juicy stems. A spring bloomer (May), the entire plant disappears by midsummer.

The plant is fairly low growing, from 12 to 18 inches high. Although not considered invasive, it will expand to form loose clumps and mats. It reseeds if conditions are favorable.

How to Start: Divisions and nursery plants are best. To grow from seed, sow only fresh seed in pots, plunge in water, then keep surface evenly moist. Plants bloom the third year from seed.

Where to Plant: Rich soil high in organic matter and with a constant moisture supply is best. With abundant watering the plant will tolerate drier soils. It grows happily in marshy areas or standing water. Give it full sun or very light shade. Plant 12 to 24 inches apart. Hardy to zone 3.

Care: Moderately easy to moderately difficult. Water abundantly and fertilize regularly. Mulch well if it is planted in exposed, dry locations. There are no serious pests. Divide to increase just after blooming is over. The plant can go for years without needing division.

Top: *Campanula carpatica*
Above: *Ceratostigma plumbaginoides.*

Campanula persicifolia (Peach-Leaf Bellflower). Harebell family. Native to Europe and Northeast Asia.

The blue or white blossoms of the peach-leaf bellflower are a charming addition to any wild garden or informal border.

The flowers are bell shaped, single or double, and spread open to 1½ inches in diameter. They appear in July on long, slender, flexible stems.

The leaves are medium green and straplike, and, as indicated by the common name, are similar to those of the peach tree.

The plant spreads outward gradually. It is restrained in growth, not invasive, and can be quite long-lived.

How to Start: Best from nursery plants or clumps divided in early spring. It also starts easily from seed sown outdoors in early spring or late summer; however, seeds seldom produce plants true to type, and considerable variation may result.

Where to Plant: As bellflower is native to mountainous meadows and open woods, the soil must be well drained and should be high in organic matter and of average fertility. Give the plant full sun or partial shade. It is best in areas with cool summers, and does not perform well in the South. Space plants 12 to 18 inches apart. Hardy to zone 3.

Care: Easy. Water regularly, as it does not tolerate prolonged drought. Feed lightly and infrequently. The tallest varieties may require staking, although this is unusual.

Crown rot can be a serious problem if water stands around the roots for any length of time. Regular applications of insecticide may be beneficial in protecting the plants from aphids and thrips.

Divide to rejuvenate when the clumps begin to decline, usually not before the third or fourth year. Division in early spring is an excellent means of increase.

Related Species: *Campanula carpatica* (Carpathian Harebell) is a low, 6- to 12-inch-high plant with large blue, purple, or white blossoms from June to August. It is neat, compact, and long-blooming, and is useful in the rock garden, in the front of the border, or as an edging. Protect from slugs.

C. glomerata (Clustered Bellflower) has very showy, large, tight clusters of violet, blue, purple, or white flowers atop erect stems. Give this plant full sun only, as in shady locations it tends to spread runners invasively. It flowers in June and July.

Ceratostigma plumbaginoides (Blue Plumbago). Leadwort family. Native to western China.

The blue plumbago is a low-growing, leafy perennial with brilliant gentian blue flowers in late summer. Its late-season blue makes it an excellent choice for beds, edging, and the front of the border.

The flowers are bright blue when they open and change to violet as they age. They appear in great quantities over the surface of the plant from August to frost.

The dark green leaves often turn a bronze red in cool fall weather. Foliage is dense and of medium to fine texture. Growing 6 to 10 inches high, the plant can spread to 18 inches, sometimes more. Masses of slender, almost prostrate stems radiate from the center, sending up many short vertical stems, each bearing flowers.

The plant spreads slowly by underground stems; in sand, the spread is rapid. It is long-lived and not invasive. Division is rarely required. Growth is slow to appear in spring; so be careful with early cultivation.

How to Start: Transplant nursery plants or clumps divided in early spring.

Where to Plant: Although not too particular about soil, the plant does best in well-drained, moist soil high in organic matter. Avoid excessively soggy or dry soils. Give it full sun or partial shade. It is highly tolerant of drought. Space plants 12 to 18 inches apart. It is hardy to zone 6, but performs well in zone 5 with a light winter mulch.

Care: It requires little attention but will respond to abundant moisture and regular fertilizing. It has no serious pests. It rarely needs division, but clumps may start to die out in the center after 3 or 4 years. This is easily corrected by division. Best performed in early spring, division is also an excellent means of increase.

Chrysanthemum coccineum 'E. M. Robinson'

Chrysanthemum coccineum (Pyrethrum; Painted Daisy). Daisy family. Native to southwestern Asia.

The painted daisy is much easier to cultivate than the hardy chrysanthemum, and blooms earlier, from June to early July. It offers daisylike flowers in intense hues of pink, white, and red, often with a contrasting eye.

The flowers are 2 to 3 inches across and are produced at the ends of long stems. They may be single or double.

The bright green, deeply dissected leaves are finely textured but relatively sparse. Stems are upright to spreading, frequently branched, and range in height from 9 inches to 3 feet, depending upon cultivar.

Painted daises form clumps that gradually increase by sending up new shoots on the outer perimeter of the crown. They are long-lived and not invasive.

How to Start: By division in late summer.

Where to Plant: Reasonably well-drained soil high in organic matter. A rich, sandy loam is best. They will not tolerate wet soil in winter. Give them full sun or very light shade. Space plants 12 to 18 inches apart. Hardy to zone 2.

Care: Moderately easy. Painted daisies tolerate moderate drought, but do best with sufficient water. They seldom need staking. Cut all stems to the ground after flowering to encourage a secondary bloom in late summer. There are no serious pests. Division usually is necessary to relieve crowding after the fourth year, and is best done in late summer. After dividing and transplanting the clump, trim the leaves in half to reduce wilting. Division is an excellent means of increase.

Chrysanthemum × morifolium (Hardy Chrysanthemum; Florist's Chrysanthemum). Daisy family. Of hybrid origin, probably from China.

Difficult to raise well, hardy chrysanthemums nevertheless can provide an outstanding show when nearly all other perennials have gone into winter dormancy. The plants offer an incredible variety of colors, sizes, and flower shapes. For the gardener with patience and attention to detail, they can yield extraordinary late-season dividends.

Flowers come in all colors except blue. Most varieties are fully double, with flowers 2 to 4 inches across (and usually larger with disbudding, described later in the entry), produced alone or in clusters at the ends of branched stems. Many forms are available, some of which are described here:

☐ *Decorative* chrysanthemums have fully double flowers with straplike "petals," or, more accurately, rays.

☐ *Pompons* produce rounded, almost spherical flowers usually 2 inches or less across.

☐ *Singles* are daisylike with an outer single or double row of rays and an often contrasting central eye.

☐ *Cushions* usually have double flowers and are distinguished by their low, bushy habit, rarely exceeding 15 inches in height.

Left: *Chrysanthemum* 'Loyalty'
Right: *Chrysanthemum* 'John Hughes'

☐ *Spoons* are oddly shaped flowers with long rays flaring out into spoon-like tips.

☐ *Commercials* are reserved largely for greenhouse growers, and are characterized by the popular, huge "football game" flowers.

☐ *Anemones* have contrasting outer rays and inner, fluffy eyes.

☐ *Buttons* are like tiny pompons an inch or less across.

☐ *Rayonettes* have a spidery, open quality with long, filamentous rays. They are often called "Spider Mums."

Hardy chrysanthemums bloom anytime from August to November, depending upon cultivar, and may bloom through December in mild climates.

The plant's overall structure differs with the many cultivars, but generally is a cluster of many-branched stems. Forms range from the low, spreading cushion mums to tall, narrow upright ones. Heights range from 1 to 4 feet. The foliage is deep green, usually dense, and attractive all season long unless damaged by pests.

The plants gradually expand outward by sending up new shoots. They are restrained in growth, never invasive, and can be long-lived if properly cared for.

How to Start: Division or stem cuttings made in late spring are the accepted methods. Do not set out young plants too early if a tall habit is not desired.

Where to Plant: Rich, fertile soil high in organic matter is best; and it is critical that the soil be perfectly drained in winter. Once established, the plants can withstand mild drought. They flower best in full sun, but usually accept partial shade well. Space plants 18 to 24 inches apart. Hardy to zone 6, and possibly zone 5 if soil is very well drained in winter.

Care: Require some effort for best appearance. Tip-pinching from spring to midsummer results in bushier, more heavily flowered plants. Start when the spring growth reaches about 6 inches, and continue each time it grows another 6 inches until mid-to-late July. Tall plants may need staking at flowering time. Feed regularly and generously throughout the growing season. Water regularly, especially over dry periods. Protect over winter with a 3- or 4-inch cover of mulch, placed after the ground is completely

Left: *Chrysanthemum* 'Charms'
Below: *Chrysanthemum* 'Seventh Heaven'

frozen, as the shallow roots are susceptible to frost heave. But guard against moisture collecting under the mulch, especially during thaws. Chrysanthemums will rot quickly in soggy, cold soil. For show, gardeners practice disbudding to achieve fewer but larger flowers. Remove all but four or five of the strongest stems in each clump, and when buds begin to show, pinch off all except the one at the top.

A wide range of bacterial, fungal, viral, and insect pests can attack the plants. Regular spraying with an all-purpose spray (containing both insecticide and fungicide) and practicing good garden sanitation are essential for healthy plants. Carefully remove and destroy any plants infected with aster yellows, foliar nematodes, or stunting (a viral disease).

Most varieties require annual division to retain vigor and good appearance, although some can get by with division every other year. This is best done in spring.

Chrysanthemum parthenium (Feverfew; Matricaria). Daisy family. Native to southeastern Europe and the Caucasus.

Tiny daisylike flowers in incredible profusion cover these low, bushy plants in July and August. White with yellow centers, the blooms come in single- and double-flowered forms.

The flowers measure from ½ to ¾ inch in diameter and appear at the ends of multibranched stems. The leaves are light green, small, and dense. In mild climates the foliage is evergreen.

Feverfew is a low, spreading plant. Most named cultivars grow 12 to 15 inches high. Seedlings can, however, eventually reach 3 feet and sprawl in an open fashion, unless pinched or sheared early in the season. Single-flower forms will self-sow everywhere; the double-flower varieties are less prolific. The species is quite long-lived, unlike the double-flower cultivars.

How to Start: Seeds sown in spring will produce flowering plants that summer. It is also easy to grow from cuttings or divisions. In fact, the smallest piece of root taken inadvertently by a spade will start a new (sometimes unwanted) plant.

Where to Plant: Feverfew tolerates many soils but performs best in sandy,

Chrysanthemum parthenium, double variety

well-drained loam. Give it full sun, although it is quite tolerant of partial shade. Space plants 12 to 24 inches apart. Hardy to zone 4.

Care: Easy, except for removing unwanted seedlings. Pinch in spring to produce denser, bushier plants. The reseeding problem tempts one to try removing flowers before they can set seed, but this is nearly impossible, as there are so many blossoms, and new ones are always appearing while others are setting seed. The plant has no serious pests. Division is seldom if ever required for rejuvenation, but is good for propagation in early spring.

Chrysanthemum × superbum (Shasta Daisy). Daisy family. Of hybrid origin; the parents probably native to Portugal and the Pyrenees.

White, daisylike flowers with a contrasting yellow eye generously cover this bushy plant all summer long.

The blossoms are 2 to 3 inches across and are produced in great profusion at the ends of strong stems. They bloom from June to frost. Single and double varieties are available.

The dark green leaves are narrow, toothed, and almost linear in shape. About an inch long, they are held close to the stem and have a fine texture. The plant is densely branched, rounded, and bushy, growing 2 to 4 feet high and as wide. The foliage will often persist well into winter; and the plant is often grown as an evergreen perennial in mild climates, where it tends to become woody at the base.

The Shasta daisy is restrained in growth and can be long-lived if located and cared for correctly.

How to Start: Best planted as a nursery plant or division in spring. Sowing seed in spring is possible, and easy, but will result in considerable variation in plants.

Where to Plant: Moist, fertile, very well-drained soil is best. It will not tolerate soggy soil in winter. Provide good air circulation and either full sun or partial shade. The double varieties show a distinct preference for partial shade in hot climates. Space plants 12 to 24 inches apart. Hardy to zone 5.

Care: Moderately easy. Water generously, especially during drought. It responds favorably to occasional feeding. Removing spent flowers will

Chrysanthemum × superbum 'Marconi'

Chrysogonum virginianum

encourage a heavier bloom. Leaf spot, stem rot, verticillium rot, and several chewing insects can be troublesome. Plants attacked by verticillium rot should be carefully removed and destroyed. Division usually is necessary every other year to restore vigor. It is best done in the spring.

Chrysogonum virginianum (Golden Star). Daisy family. Native from Pennsylvania to Florida and Louisiana.

Golden star is a low, trailing plant with small, daisylike, bright yellow flowers and vivid green leaves. It is useful either in sun or shade, and is particularly delightful when grown against or around rocks.

The flowers appear from mid-June to frost and are produced along the joints of trailing, leafy stems. The bright green leaves are small and round, about an inch across, and dense. Most varieties sold commercially have gray-green foliage.

The plant has a loose, open habit that follows the contour of the ground and rocks. It usually grows 2 to 4 inches high, and rarely exceeds 8 inches. It often spreads into a loose mat with stems rooting where they touch the soil. Golden star is always restrained in growth and never intrusive, seldom exceeding a spread of 12 to 20 inches.

How to Start: Best started in early spring from divisions or nursery container plants. It is possible to start from seed sown in late spring or late summer, but expect considerable variation in leaf size and leaf color.

Where to Plant: Chrysogonum must have excellent drainage and preferably a sandy soil high in organic matter. Give it either full sun or partial shade. The soil should be fairly dry and of only average fertility. Space plants 8 to 12 inches apart. Hardy to zone 3.

Care: Moderately easy. Removing spent flowers before they can set seed will prolong bloom. Water moderately during periods of drought. There are no serious pests. Divide in early spring for increase. The plant rarely if ever requires division for rejuvenation.

Cimicifuga racemosa (Black Snakeroot; Bugbane). Buttercup family. Native from Massachusetts to Ontario, south to Georgia, Tennessee, and Missouri.

The black snakeroot produces tall, thin, exceedingly graceful spires of

Cimicifuga racemosa with *Achillea* and *Echinops*

white, fluffy flowers, sometimes reaching to 8 feet above the foliage clumps. It is excellent in the rear of the border.

Open and airy in bloom, the wandlike flower stalks sway with each breeze. The flowers are small and are produced densely along the upper part of the stalks, in racemes up to 3 feet long. They are vertical and graceful, and exude a cloying sweet fragrance. Peak flowering occurs in late June and July, but small lateral branches bear flowers into August.

The glistening dark green leaves are compound, divided into three toothed leaflets. The foliage forms dense clumps 2 to 3 feet high and provides good color until frost.

Black snakeroot does not self-sow freely or spread about the garden and can never be considered intrusive. The rhizomes expand slowly to increase the clump. The plant is very long-lived.

How to Start: Division in early spring or container-grown nursery plants with well-developed root systems are best. To plant a bare-root clump from a division, place the rhizome (one with at least two eyes) so that the eyes are exactly 1 inch below soil level. Seeds may be collected and sown in the fall. To sow in spring, prechill in the refrigerator for several weeks. Sow at 45° to 50°. Germination is slow and erratic.

Where to Plant: Since the plant is native to the deep, rich, moist soils of open woodlands and the forest edge, it is best in moist, well-drained soil high in organic matter. It grows tallest in deep soil and filtered shade, and ideally should not have more than 4 hours of direct sun each day. In deep shade, however, it will not flower well. Hardy to zone 3.

Care: Moderately easy. Water abundantly and fertilize regularly. The plant prefers cool soil, and it is best to mulch deeply throughout the summer. Division is an excellent means of increase, but is rarely required for rejuvenation. Clumps can go for many years left alone.

Related Species: *Cimicifuga americana* is native to North America. Its foliage is more open and appears higher up the stalks. A smaller species, growing 2 to 4 feet tall, it blooms from August into September or October.

C. dahurica is native to eastern Asia. Its foliage is coarser, and it never exceeds 4 or 5 feet in height. It blooms from August into fall.

C. foetida is more branched at the base, grows from 18 to 36 inches high, and blooms in September and October.

Coreopsis lanceolata (Perennial Coreopsis). Daisy family. Native from Michigan south to Florida and New Mexico.

This perennial coreopsis produces bright golden yellow "daisies" on long stems above tufted, leafy mounds all summer long. They are most useful at the front or middle of the border.

The flowers have yellow "petals," actually ray flowers, with yellow or brown centers. They are about 3 inches wide and are produced in abundance on long stems in June through September.

The dark green leaves are long and straplike. The basal mounds, or tufts, of leaves support many flower stalks reaching to 2 feet high.

Although it often reseeds, perennial coreopsis is seldom invasive like its annual cousins. It is long-lived, and the clumps expand slowly from the center. Do not confuse this plant with several cultivars hybridized from *Coreopsis grandiflora*, as those are short-lived perennials.

How to Start: Easy to start from seed, and most cultivars will breed true to type. Sow outdoors in spring or summer up to 2 months prior to the first frost; or, for flowers the first year, sow indoors 6 to 8 weeks ahead of the last frost in spring. Keep the germinating medium at 60° to 70°, and do not cover the seeds. The plant is also easy to start by clump division in spring.

Coreopsis verticillata 'Golden Shower'

Where to Plant: The plant is extremely tolerant; give it any well-drained soil in full sun. Space them 12 inches apart. Hardy to zone 3.

Care: Easy. Water through dry periods and feed occasionally. For the longest bloom period, and to prevent reseeding, remove faded flowers before they can set seed. Leaf spot, rust, and powdery mildew can be severe problems. Foliage may also require protection from several chewing insects. While clumps can go for many years before requiring division to rejuvenate, it is an excellent means of increase in early spring.

Related Species: *Coreopsis grandiflora* is a short-lived perennial and a weedy self-sower. It has a shorter bloom season, from mid-June through July.

C. verticillata (Threadleaf Coreopsis) is full, bushy, and grows to 3 feet tall. Its dense foliage is exceedingly fine in texture, misty, and soft in appearance. The plant is covered with small golden flowers all summer. While not invasive, it performs best with frequent division. Of all coreopsis it is the most tolerant of dry soils. Threadleaf coreopsis is easy, restrained in growth, and long-lived.

Delphinium elatum (Delphinium). Buttercup family. Native from central and southern Europe to Siberia.

Famous for their tall, bold spikes in rich blues, delphiniums are tricky flowers to cultivate well. Much frustration has resulted from seeing pictures of these magnificent plants as raised in England, for there are not many areas of this country so conducive to their good growth. When grown well, however, they have few rivals for their dramatic effect at the rear of the border.

The flowers are mostly blue, but also come in pink, white, red, violet, and purple. Individually they are spurred and solid or often bicolored, with a contrasting white or black eye, sometimes called a "bee." Borne profusely and densely along tall, vertical spikes, they bloom from June into July.

The dark green leaves are lobed and medium-coarse in texture. They are large and dense at the base, smaller and sparser higher up. The stiffly erect stems appear in clumps and are usually about 4 feet tall; under optimum conditions, however, they can reach 7 or 8 feet or more in height. Size also varies according to cultivar. The flowers are produced along the upper third or fourth of each stem, in dense vertical spikes.

Delphiniums are usually short-lived, often being treated as a biennial or a short-lived perennial. Under the best conditions, the clumps will expand

Delphinium elatum

gradually and the stems will grow in height and number as the years progress.

How to Start: The most successful method is to start from container-grown plants purchased from the nursery either in early spring or early fall. Or start from divisions made in early spring, being sure to dust all cut surfaces with a fungicide. Avoid planting young starts or divisions too deeply. The plant can be started by seed sown outdoors in spring or summer. Or sow indoors, completely covered, at a temperature of 55° to 65°.

Where to Plant: Soil must be rich, moist, well drained, and high in organic matter. It should be slightly alkaline, or at least neutral. Provide full sun and good air circulation. Originally native to the cool mountain meadows of Europe to Siberia, delphiniums will decline rapidly in regions with hot, muggy summers. Space plants 18 to 36 inches apart. Hardy to zone 2.

Care: Difficult, but the effort is worthwhile. Fertilize with a 5-10-10 fertilizer in early spring and again later during the growing season. Water abundantly but never let the soil remain soggy; and try not to get any moisture on the leaves. Staking is absolutely necessary to prevent the heavy spikes from breaking in the wind, and the shallow-rooted plants from dislodging from the soil. Because the roots are shallow and delicate, cultivate gently. As flowers fade, snip off the spike just below the lowest blossom. When the new growth from the base reaches 6 inches, cut the old stem clear to the ground. This will produce a second, though less spectacular, flowering season in late summer.

Powdery mildew, crown rot, and several other fungal pests are problems, as are many insects, snails, and slugs. Applying both a fungicide and an insecticide at 10-day intervals is strongly advised. Remove and destroy all infected plants, and do not replant in the same area where crown rot has attacked. Protect the crowns from snails and slugs in fall and early spring. Mulch well after the ground freezes.

In favorable locations where they live long, delphiniums should be divided after every third or fourth year. This is best done in early spring just as the new growth appears. Dust all cut surfaces with fungicide.

Related Species: *Delphinium × belladonna* is a shorter hybrid and is much longer-lived.

Dianthus plumarius (Cottage Pink; Scotch Pink). Pink family. Native to central Europe.

Cottage pinks produce rose, pink, red, or white blossoms in spring on tufted, compact plants. Their gray-green leaves often persist through winter.

The flowers are about 1½ inches wide, fringed, and lacy, and can be solid or bicolored, single or double. They appear in great quantities above the narrow, grasslike foliage, blooming in May and June.

The foliage forms dense mats 6 to 8 inches high, and the flower stems extend the height to a total of 12 inches. The mats will expand gradually and indefinitely. Cottage pink will self-sow, but is seldom invasive. Under favorable conditions, it is hardy and long-lived.

How to Start: Divisions or nursery plants are most frequently used. It is also easily grown from cuttings in the spring. The plant is easy to start from seed, but this will result in considerable variation.

Where to Plant: Sharply drained soil, preferably on the alkaline side. It performs best in sandy soil amended with organic matter to retain moisture during the dry seasons. Give it full sun and good air circulation. Most cottage pinks are not for southern climates with hot, muggy summers, and do best in cool coastal or mountainous areas of northern latitudes. Space plants 12 to 15 inches apart. Hardy to zone 3.

Care: Moderately easy. Water during drought. Shear the flowers toward the end of the blooming season to encourage new growth and prevent reseeding. Leaf spot may become a problem in muggy weather or in crowded conditions. Apply a fungicide as soon as it is detected. Division is best performed in early spring and is one of the best means of increase. It also may be necessary every third or fourth year to prevent overcrowding.

Related Species and Hybrids: *Dianthus × allwoodii* is a hybrid strain generally agreed to be derived from crosses between the carnation and the cottage pink. The foliage is a bit coarser and the plant stockier than *D. plumarius,* growing to about 12 inches tall. It is reportedly more tolerant of the hot, muggy summers of the Southeast.

   D. caryophyllus (Carnation) includes types sold as annuals; but, although they are among the most tender of the species, all are true perennials. The hardiest border carnations will often survive temperatures as low as 12° if protected by evergreen boughs. They are quite fragrant, much more so than greenhouse carnations.

   D. deltoides (Maiden Pink) is a low-growing, mat-forming species with small, profuse flowers in June. The turflike foliage is semievergreen, often turning blackish and persisting throughout the winter.

Dicentra spectabilis (Bleeding Heart). Dutchman's Breeches family. Native to Japan.

The flowers of the bleeding heart are aptly named. They are puffy and suggest a heart with two "drops of blood" flaring up and out from the base, resulting in an overall lyre shape. The blossoms are rose-pink with white tips, pink, or occasionally white in color, and hang pendulously from horizontally arching and drooping stems. The racemes are up to 9 inches long, and are produced among and on top of the foliage.

   The foliage is medium green, often with a slightly grayish cast, with deeply cut leaves that give the plant a finely textured appearance. The plant forms dense clumps of arching sprays of foliage 30 inches tall and up to 36 inches wide. Because of its relatively large size and a tendency to die down after blooming, it is best used as a specimen rather than massed, and used with accompanying plants that will take its place later in the season. It is an especially excellent specimen plant in partial shade.

How to Start: Young plants purchased from a nursery are best planted in the spring before the new growth starts. Bleeding heart can be started from

Dianthus plumarius

Dicentra spectabilis

seed, but this requires patience. Sow seed outdoors in late fall or early winter, or start indoors by sowing them in small flats, freezing them for 6 weeks, then taking them out and germinating at 55° to 60°. Seedlings should appear in 3 to 5 weeks.

Where to Plant: The plant prefers rich, moist, well-drained soil high in organic matter; and partial shade. It will tolerate full sun or deep shade quite well; however, in full sun the foliage is likely to burn and die back quickly after flowering. It is also best to keep the plant out of drying winds. Space plants 2 feet apart if not growing as a single specimen. Hardy to zone 2.

Care: Easy to moderately easy. Water abundantly and feed regularly, but cut back when the dormant period begins. Cultivars advertised as "blooming all summer" require the regular removal of spent blossoms. The chief problem is stem rot, which is caused by soggy soil and poor drainage. It is best not to disturb this plant; division is seldom successful and not necessary.

Related Species and Varieties: *Dicentra eximea* (Fringed Bleeding Heart) is notable for its beautiful gray-green, finely dissected foliage, which contrasts effectively with its deep rose-to-white flowers. It also has a longer flowering season. Several hybrid forms of this plant (probably crosses with *D. formosa*, among others) will bloom intermittently all summer long if faded blossoms are removed. One example is the beautiful hybrid 'Bountiful', which bears intense, deep red flowers off and on from June until frost.

   D. formosa (Western Bleeding Heart) is an aggressive spreader with flower stems about 1 foot tall and blossoms rose-purple to white in color.

Dictamnus albus (Gas Plant). Citrus family. Native from southern Europe to northern China.

The gas plant is a large, bushy perennial with showy flowers in early summer and excellent, clean, long-lasting foliage useful as a background. A lit match held just below a blossom will ignite the minute amount of gas it releases with a soft "pop," and no injury to the flower.

   The flowers are white, pink, or purplish. Individually, they are irregular and small, about 1 inch across, but are produced in great quantities on spikes at the top of the plant. They bloom in late May and June.

   The foliage is medium green, dense, and of medium texture, and remains attractive until frost. When the leaves are brushed or crushed, they exude the fragrance of lemons, to which the plant is related.

Dictamnus albus

   Gas plant forms dense clumps of vertical and slightly arching stems with many lateral branches. It grows to 3 feet high, and with age often spreads twice as wide, the clumps gradually enlarging by expanding rhizomes. It is quite long-lived.

How to Start: Setting out young nursery plants is by far the most common method. This should be done in spring. To start from seed, sow outdoors in late fall or early winter. They will germinate the following spring, but it is best to wait another year to transplant them. Seedlings do not take well to transplanting, so it is better to plant in individual pots.

Where to Plant: This plant prefers rich, well-drained soil high in organic matter. Avoid wet, soggy soils. Give it full sun or light shade. Allow 3 feet on all sides. Hardy to zone 2.

Care: Easy. Gas plant responds to occasional feeding during the growing season. It has no serious pests. Division is never necessary and if tried is seldom successful. It resents transplanting and disturbance.

Related Species and Cultivars: *Dictamnus albus*, the species, has pure white flowers.

   D. albus 'Purpureus' has deep pink flowers. *D. albus* 'Rubra' has rosy-purple flowers.

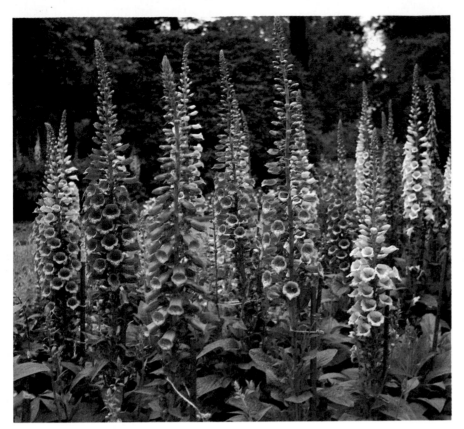

Digitalis purpurea Excelsior hybrids

Digitalis purpurea (Foxglove). Snapdragon family. Native to the western Mediterranean region.

While a true biennial, the foxglove self-sows generously, and is thus usually considered a permanent fixture in the garden. The tall spikes of colorful flowers atop leafy stems lend an outstanding vertical effect, most valuable at the rear of the border. The plant is also excellent for informal, naturalistic plantings.

Flowers are purple, pink, white, reddish, or yellow, often with a spotted throat. Individually they are tubular, about 2½ inches long, inclined at a downward tilt, and are produced along one side of tall, erect stems. Each raceme of flowers, often 1 or 2 feet long, starts blooming at the base and ends at the top. They appear in June and July.

How the plant arrived at its common name is open to question. Apart from the common notion that it refers to gloves for a fox, some contend that the word is derived from "folks' gloves," referring to gloves wearable by fairies ("folks"). Others believe that it is a corruption of "folks' *glauve*," which in medieval English meant a hand-held set of bells (glauve) of a size appropriate to fairies.

The leaves are large, somewhat rough and wrinkled, and dark green on the upper surface and light green beneath, where they are covered with whitish hairs. They are dense at the base of the plant, becoming smaller and more scarce toward the top.

Foxglove grows 2 to 5 feet tall. It is biennial, and will sometimes bloom a second time with smaller spikes if the flowers are removed before they can set seed. The plant self-sows abundantly, but cannot be relied upon to do so unless conditions are favorable. The foliage tends to look unattractive after blooming is complete.

How to Start: Plant nursery plants in spring. Or sow outdoors in late spring or early summer, or indoors at a constant temperature of 70°. Do not cover the seeds. Germination occurs in 1 to 3 weeks.

Where to Plant: Acid, moist, well-drained soil high in organic matter. The plant is partial to deep shade, but tolerates full sun. Hybrid varieties are usually less particular about soil. Space plants 18 to 24 inches apart. Hardy to zone 4.

Care: Moderately easy. Removing flower spikes before they set seed will encourage second-year bloom, but it will be inferior. Otherwise allow the plants to self-sow and remove unattractive plants after their seed is dispersed. Regular applications of fungicide to protect from powdery mildew and leaf spot, and of insecticide to protect from aphids, mealybugs, and Japanese beetles, may prove beneficial. Division is not applicable, as the plants usually die after they flower.

Related Species and Cultivars: The Excelsior Hybrids are the best choice, because they produce flowers on all sides of the stem. The flowers are so tightly packed that they do not droop, as does the species, but are held at right angles to the stem. They come in pastel shades of pink, white, yellow, and rose, usually in mixes.

There are some truly perennial species of foxglove, but they have fewer and less colorful flowers.

Doronicum cordatum (Leopard's Bane). Daisy family. Native to southeastern Europe and Western Asia.

The spring-blooming, daisylike, bright yellow flowers of leopard's bane appear in great quantities above clusters of large, heart-shaped leaves.

Each blossom is 2 to 3 inches across and appears on its own 9- to 15-inch stem. The plant blooms in May, and the foliage declines and often dies down after flowering is complete.

The foliage is of medium to coarse texture and is produced in low basal clumps of 3- to 5-inch leaves, medium to bright green in color. The clumps grow 8 to 12 inches high, and with flowers the plant often reaches 2 to 3 feet in height, spreading nearly as wide.

Leopard's bane produces shallow, dense, fibrous roots. The clumps expand rapidly and start dying out in the center unless divided. Since the foliage dies out early in the season, the plant is best used as a specimen rather than massed, and should be combined with other plants that will fill

Doronicum cordatum

in the empty space. In warm climates with long, mild autumns, the foliage may come back and the plant bloom again.

How to Start: Nursery plants or divisions, taken in August while the plant is dormant. Or sow seed outdoors in late spring or summer. Germination is slow and erratic, but usually occurs within 4 weeks.

Where to Plant: Rich, moist soil high in organic matter. It prefers partial shade, especially in hot climates. Space plants 12 to 15 inches apart. Hardy to zone 4.

Care: Easy. Water moderately during the growing season. There are no serious pests. Division for rejuvenation is usually required every 2 to 4 years, and is best done during dormancy in August or very early spring. It is also an excellent means of increase.

Echinacea purpurea (Purple Coneflower). Daisy family. Native from Ohio to Iowa, south to Louisiana and Georgia.

The purple coneflower is a large, coarse plant with daisylike flowers that have relaxed, drooping "petals." Named cultivars are much superior to the species.

Echinacea purpurea 'Bright Star'

The flowers come in purple and, occasionally, white. The "petals," technically ray flowers, droop back toward the stem. The eye is conical, bristly, and colored with purple, maroon, or brown. The "flowers" (flower heads) are 3 to 4 inches wide and appear at the ends of many long, branched stems. They bloom from July to September.

The foliage is dull green and composed of large, coarse-textured leaves that are dense at the base of the plant, smaller and more scattered toward the top. The plant forms a clump of many stems, which are branched, semi-erect, and spreading.

Purple coneflower grows 3 to 5 feet high and 2 to 5 feet wide. It is long-lived and not invasive.

How to Start: Divisions or started root cuttings from a nursery. Seeds will not produce plants true to type, but will result in many inferior plants.

Where to Plant: Soil should be sandy and well drained. Provide full sun or light shade; the latter produces richer colors. The plant is native to North American prairies and meadows, mostly at the edges of woods. It is drought and wind tolerant. Space plants 18 to 24 inches apart. Hardy to zone 3.

Care: Moderately easy. It responds to light feeding and moderate watering. Never allow the soil to remain soggy. Japanese beetles can ruin this plant very quickly; protect it with traps or insecticide. Clumps will require division every third or fourth year for rejuvenation. This is also an excellent means of increase, and should be performed in early spring just as new growth appears.

Cultivars: It is best to purchase named cultivars, as most have bigger flowers and better color than the species.

'The King' is probably the most famous hybrid. Its 6-inch flowers are brilliant reddish purple with brown centers. It grows to 3 feet and has a more refined appearance.

'White Lustre' has creamy white flowers that are produced in incredible profusion, even in severe drought. Its foliage and structure, however, are quite coarse.

Echinops exaltatus (Globe Thistle). Daisy family. Native to Russia.

Globe thistles are large, bold plants with round flower heads and spiny, toothed leaves.

The flowers, which bloom in July through August, are various shades of blue. Individually tiny, they are gathered into dense, bristly balls about

Top: *Echinops exaltatus* 'Veitch's Blue'
Above: *Echinops exaltatus* 'Blue Globe'

Erigeron speciosus

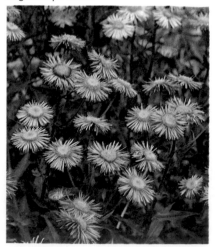

2 inches across. These balls occur singly at the ends of branched stems, and dry well for winter flower arrangements.

The leaves are deep green on the upper surface and white on the lower. Deeply toothed, they have a coarse appearance. The plant produces dense clumps of semi-erect, spreading stems. The clumps expand gradually and require periodic thinning. However, the roots are dense and about 1 foot deep, and thus difficult to divide. The plants tend to lose leaves at the base as the season progresses.

How to Start: Divisions or young container plants from a nursery are best. Always be sure to acquire named cultivars. Plant in early spring. Seedlings are extremely variable and usually inferior.

Where to Plant: Well-drained soil of only average fertility. Rich soil will produce taller, more open plants. Full sun is best, but the plant tolerates partial shade. It withstands considerable drought, but responds to adequate moisture. It does very poorly in soggy soil. Space plants 18 to 24 inches apart. Hardy to zone 3.

Care: Moderately easy. Globe thistle requires little special attention and has no serious pests. Although difficult due to the deep and extensive root system, division is necessary every third or fourth year. It is an excellent means of increase, and is best done in early spring.

Cultivars: The best cultivar is 'Taplow Blue', which has steel-blue, 3-inch flower heads.

Erigeron speciosus (Oregon Fleabane). Daisy family. Northwestern North America.

The Oregon fleabane is a small, tidy plant with multitudes of asterlike flowers. It blooms in June and early July, and is most useful in groups of 3 or more in the front of the border.

The flowers are violet, lavender, pink, or mauve, with yellow centers. They have extremely narrow petals, are 1 to 2 inches across, and appear singly at the ends of the stems. If spent flowers are continually removed, the flowering season may extend sporadically into September.

The foliage is dull green and thick at the base, becoming thinner along the branching, semi-erect, and spreading stems. Leaves are lance-shaped and medium in texture. The plant forms clumps 1½ to 2 feet high. They gradually overcrowd and die out in the center. Oregon fleabane can be long-lived, however, if divided occasionally. It is never invasive.

How to Start: Nursery plants or divisions are best. Try always to acquire named cultivars that have been propagated vegetatively, as inferior plants result from seed.

Where to Plant: Relatively dry, infertile soil low in organic matter and with excellent drainage. The plant will not tolerate soggy, wet soil. Give it full sun. Space plants 12 inches apart. Hardy to zone 3.

Care: Moderately easy. Little special attention is needed in the correct planting site. Removing faded flowers before they can set seed will prolong flowering, but this can be time-consuming, as bloom is profuse. Mildew, leaf spot, rust, and aphids can be problems, especially in overly moist soil and in humid environments. The plant will require rejuvenation by division every third or fourth year. Division in early spring is an excellent means of increase.

Eryngium amethystinum (Sea Holly). Parsley family. Native to Europe.

The curious, interesting flower heads of the sea holly are composed of ovoid tufts surrounded by spiny, leafy bracts. The whole flower structure is an unusual metallic blue-gray in color.

A half-inch to an inch long, the flowers bloom in July and August and appear in large quantities at the ends of multibranched, bluish stems. They dry well, retaining their color, and are excellent for winter arrangements.

The foliage is deep green, deeply cut, bristly, and medium-coarse in texture. Many stems branch low to the ground, resulting in a bushy, spreading plant 1½ to 2 feet tall. It develops a deep tap root that makes division difficult.

The plant will self-sow freely, and is long-lived if the soil is well drained and dry during winter. It is an excellent choice for sandy, infertile soils, especially in seaside gardens.

How to Start: Most commonly from young nursery plants started as root cuttings. To start from seed, prechill the seed in the refrigerator for several weeks prior to spring planting. Germination can be erratic and slow; sprouts may not appear until the following year. Starting from divisions is possible, but difficult.

Where to Plant: It does best in sandy, well-drained soil, but tolerates

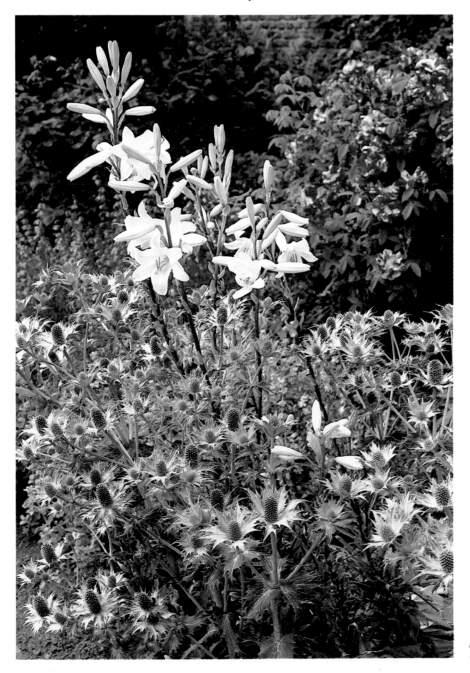

Eryngium amethystinum with white lilies and roses

heavier soils as long as they are dry over winter. Give it full sun. Space plants 12 to 18 inches apart. Hardy to zone 6.

Care: Easy. It never needs staking and has no serious pests. Sea holly should not be disturbed once established, since it reacts unfavorably to transplanting. Division is further complicated due to the long tap root. It is possible, however, and often successful if performed carefully in early spring.

Related Species: *Eryngium alpinum* is a smaller plant, never exceeding 18 inches high, whose bracts are a beautiful metallic silvery blue, and whose stems are a deep, rich indigo. It is, unfortunately, rarely available.

Euphorbia epithymoides, formerly *E. polychroma* (Cushion Spurge). Spurge family. Native to eastern Europe.

The bright yellow-green floral bracts in spring, an excellent, neat, mounded habit, and clean foliage all summer long make this plant attractive as a specimen or at the front of the border.

The true flowers are minute and yellow, but each is surrounded by large, leafy, bright chartreuse bracts. Flowers appear in late April to early June.

The dark green leaves, covered with whitish hairs, turn a rich dark red in fall. Of medium texture, the foliage is pest-free and attractive all season. The plant is thick with leaves held tightly against the stems, forming a dense mound 1 to 2 feet high.

The plant is more restrained in growth and less invasive than some other spurges; however, it will self-sow. Cushion spurge is long-lived.

How to Start: Young nursery plants should be set out in early spring. It is also easy to start from seed sown outdoors in late fall or early spring.

Where to Plant: The plant tolerates nearly any soil, but can spread invasively if soil is rich and moist. It will take dry, poor soils and remain in excellent condition. Give it full sun. The neat, symmetrical habit is best as a specimen, but if planted in groups, space them 12 to 15 inches apart. Hardy to zone 4.

Euphorbia epithymoides

Filipendula rubra

Care: Easy. Spurges are quite tolerant of drought, heat, and neglect. There are no serious pests. It resents disturbance and does not transplant well. In rich, moist soil, careful division in either spring or fall may be necessary to check excessive spreading.

Related Species: *Euphorbia corollata* (Flowering Spurge) is quite unlike cushion spurge. It produces misty sprays of tiny white flowers, resembling baby's breath, in July and August; and the foliage turns a deep red in fall. It self-sows plentifully, is extremely tough and adaptable, and never needs staking.

E. *cyparissias* (Cypress Spurge) is low, bushy, and mat-forming. It has narrow, linear leaves of fine texture, and yellow-green floral bracts in May and June. It is best planted in dry, poor soil, such as in a stony bank, as it will become a rampant weed in soil of even average fertility and moisture.

E. *myrsinites* (Myrtle Euphorbia) is evergreen and very hardy. The gray-green foliage is produced on trailing, fleshy stems only 3 to 6 inches high and over a foot long. It tends to spread invasively by creeping, rooting stems, and by massive seed production. It can be excellent, however, trailing down a rock wall or as a ground cover in dry, poor soil. It is the most highly recommended spurge for the Deep South.

Filipendula rubra (Queen of the Prairie). Rose family. Native from Pennsylvania to Iowa, and south to Georgia and Kentucky.

This is a tall, stately plant with large, feathery pink plumes in midsummer and lush foliage that remains attractive all season. It is a fine choice for the rear of the border.

The individual flowers are tiny, but together form plumes at the ends of the stems. The effect is delicate and finely textured. Flowers appear in late June through July.

The medium green, compound leaves are dense and lush. The plant produces clumps of numerous erect, leafy stems 4 to 6 feet high, each bearing flowers at the top. The clumps expand gradually by slowly creeping rhizomes. It is restrained in growth, never invasive, and long-lived.

How to Start: Nursery plants or divisions made in spring. If started by seed, it must be fresh and should be sown outdoors in early fall.

Where to Plant: Since its native habitat is the moist, deep soil of bottomland prairies and meadows, plant the queen of the prairie in fertile, moist soil high in organic matter. It flowers best in full sun, but is quite tolerant of partial shade. Space plants 12 to 24 inches apart. Hardy to zone 3.

Care: Moderately easy. Water abundantly and feed regularly. During wet or humid weather mildew may present a problem. Control with fungicide. While the plant seldom requires division for rejuvenation, it is an excellent means of increase. Divide in early spring just as the new growth begins.

Related Species and Varieties: *Filipendula vulgaris* (Dropwort) grows only to 2 feet. Misty clusters of ivory flowers, single or double, appear in June and are held above finely textured, ferny foliage. It withstands drought and poor soil better than other filipendulas, and is the best choice for the Southeast, where the foliage frequently is evergreen. The double 'Flore Pleno' cultivar flowers longer than the species.

  F. rubra 'Venusta' (Martha Washington Plume) is superior to the species, with huge, 12-inch, feathery plumes that are deep, bright pink. It blooms in July and early August.

  F. ulmaria (Queen of the Meadow) is similar to *F. rubra* except that the flowers are white. Growing to 4 feet, it blooms in June to mid-July.

Gaillardia × *grandiflora* (Blanket Flower). Daisy family. Of hybrid origin, parents native to the mountainous West and the Southeast in the United States.

The blanket flower is a relatively short-lived perennial with bright red, bronze, or yellow flowers, often in combination. Best planted in the front of the border in groups of 3 or more, it provides bloom all summer long.

  The daisylike flowers have outer rays that can be solid or bicolored, and a central eye that can be yellow, brown, or purple. They are 3 to 4 inches across, and appear at the ends of leafy stems in great quantities, blooming from June to September.

  The foliage is dark green, dense, and of medium texture, with hairy, lance-shaped leaves. Gaillardia forms clumps of multibranched, erect to spreading stems, and can grow to 3 feet tall. The plant spreads outward by underground rhizomes. It is usually quite short-lived.

How to Start: Easiest by nursery plants or divisions made in early spring. Named varieties purchased as young plants from the nursery are usually root cuttings. Plants usually do not come true from seed, but to start by seed, sow outdoors in early spring or summer for flowering plants the next season. Or sow indoors in late winter at a constant 70°. Do not cover seed, as it requires light to germinate.

Where to Plant: Soil must be very well drained and of average to poor fertility. Rich, moist soils, especially if wet over winter, lead to an open, sprawling habit and an early death. Give it full sun. It tolerates heat and drought well. Space plants 10 to 15 inches apart. Hardy to zone 2.

Care: Do not overwater or overfertilize gaillardia. Remove spent flowers before they can set seed to prolong the flowering period. Taller plants may require staking.

  A regular program of both insecticide and fungicide will help prevent leaf spot, powdery mildew, aster yellows, and damage from various sucking insects. Carefully remove and destroy any plant infected with aster yellows.

  Blanket flower requires annual division to perpetuate blooming from year to year. During the summer, prune roots by inserting a spade in a circle 6 inches around the crown. This stimulates the production of new plants from the severed roots. Transplant these in early spring. This process should be performed annually, as the plants are short-lived.

Gaillardia × *grandiflora* 'Goblin'

Geranium sanguineum (Bloodred Geranium). Geranium family. Native to Eurasia.

The bloodred geranium (named for its fall foliage color) is a hardy herbaceous perennial with deeply cut leaves, a mounded, spreading form, and small, single magenta flowers. It should not be confused with the tender perennial or annual *Pelargonium*, which is often called geranium in the trade.

Flower varieties come in purplish-pink, red, or white. The blossoms are from 1 to 2 inches wide, have five petals, and appear at the ends of stems rising to 8 inches above the foliage. They bloom in May to August.

The bright green leaves have five lobes, are medium to fine in texture, and turn a bright red in the fall. The plant forms dense mounds up to 2 feet wide, 1½ feet tall. It is long-lived, and may spread and self-sow invasively.

How to Start: Sow fresh seed outdoors in early spring, or indoors at a constant 70°. Germination should occur in 1 to 5 weeks. Starting by divisions made in spring, or stem cuttings made in summer, can be equally successful.

Where to Plant: Geraniums adapt to most soils, except wet or very dry ones, and are best with good drainage. Give them either full sun or partial shade. Soils of only average fertility are best; rich, moist soils promote invasive growth. Space plants 12 inches apart. Hardy to zone 3.

Care: Moderately easy. Do not overfertilize. The plant is little disturbed by pests, but the four-lined plant bug has been reported a problem. Bloodred geranium will require rejuvenation by division every 3 or 4 years. This is also an excellent means of increase, and should be done in spring.

Related Species and Varieties: *Geranium endressii* grows 15 to 18 inches high, and is best known for its cultivars 'Johnson's Blue', with light gentian-blue flowers; and 'Wargrave Pink', with clear pink flowers. Both plants will flower over a long season, nearly all summer, if cut back after the first wave of blooms in May.

G. himalayense (Lilac Cranesbill), formerly *G. grandiflorum*, has blue, purple, or lavender flowers during May and July on 2-foot, mounded, spreading plants.

G. sanguineum var. *prostratum* (formerly called *G. lancastrense*) is more restrained and neat in growth habit than the species, seldom taller than 6 or 8 inches, with bright rose-pink blossoms nearly all summer long.

Geum hybrids (Geum; Avens). Rose family. The various parents are native to the colder temperate regions in both the northern and southern hemispheres.

The many hybrid forms of geum produce long, branching stems bearing flowers in bright reds, oranges, and yellows, often in electric hues. They are attractive both as specimens and in the mixed border.

The flowers are small, up to about 1 inch across, and single, with double and semidouble cultivars. They appear in great profusion in May to August, and even longer if spent flowers are removed before they can set seed.

The stems and flowers radiate in all directions from dense basal clumps of large, deep-green leaves. Irregular and toothed, the leaves also appear on the 24- to 30-inch stems, becoming smaller and fewer as they ascend. The stems are multibranched and open.

While all avens grow slowly, the newer hybrids are even slower to increase; however, they are also longer-lived. The plants are never invasive.

How to Start: The best results come with named cultivars from nursery plants or divisions made in late summer. The latter will usually bloom the next spring. They are also easily started from seed sown outdoors in spring

Geranium himalayense

Geum coccineum 'Red Wings'

or summer, but the hybrids will not breed true, and considerable variation will result. The germination rate is poor, so sow thickly.

Where to Plant: The plant is quite choosy about location. The soil must have excellent drainage and a reasonable amount of organic matter. Water abundantly during the growing season, but avoid wet soil in winter; it is fatal. Give it full sun. It is reliably hardy to very low temperatures if the soil is dry, and performs best in regions of cool summers. Space plants 12 to 18 inches apart. Hardy to zone 5.

Care: Moderately difficult unless planted correctly; otherwise, they need little attention. Remove spent flowers to keep plants neat and extend bloom into fall. Avens has no serious pests. Division is an excellent means of increase, and is best done in late summer. The older cultivars will require division every other year, but the newer hybrids can often go for many years before needing rejuvenation.

Grasses, ornamental

Arrhenatherum elatius **'Variegatum'** (Variegated Bulbous Oatgrass). This grass is loosely tufted and deciduous, with attractive, striped leaves that have a clean white margin. When in flower (June to September) the plants may reach 3 feet in height and spread. This cultivar may be invasive, especially in rich soils, but is still more restrained in growth than the species. It is easy to grow in rich soil and either full sun or partial shade. In hot weather the foliage may brown and turn unsightly; it is often recommended to cut this grass back once about midsummer. Divide every 2 to 3 years to maintain vigor. It is native to the grasslands of Europe and Western Asia, and is hardy to zone 5.

Calamagrostis epigeios **'Hortorum',** also listed as *Calamagrostis* × *acutiflora* **'Stricta'** (Reed Grass). This cultivar of reed grass is considered indispensable by many advanced gardeners for its narrowly vertical habit from 3 to 6 feet tall. Rich, foxy, golden-red inflorescences that are attractive all winter long, begin blooming in late June and July, which is quite early for most grasses. It is easy to grow in any fertile soil and full sun, as long as it is kept moist. Reed grass is one of the few grasses that will thrive in heavy, wet clay soil, and actually prefers boggy situations. In light, sandy, moist soil it may become invasive by creeping rhizomes. Reed grass is native discontinuously from Northern Europe to East and South Africa. It is hardy to zone 5.

Cortaderia selloana (Pampas Grass). Perennial only in mild climates (zone 7 and south), this large, coarse grass often establishes huge clumps from 4 to 20 feet high. It is upright and spreading to mounded in form, with huge, fluffy plumes of flowers up to 3 feet long atop the tall stems. The flowers can be whitish or buff in color, or a pale pink, and they appear in the fall (summer in the mildest climates). Pampas grass performs quite well in dry, poor soils, but fertile moist ones are best. It prefers full sun. Occasionally dwarf or pink selections are offered. A new cultivar with yellow-variegated leaves, 'Gold Band', has recently been introduced.

C. *jubata* is another species that is occasionally encountered in the trade, usually mistakenly identified as C. *selloana*. C. *jubata* spreads profusely and likely will become an overgrowing pest, especially in the milder climates of the West Coast. Unfortunately, it is extremely difficult to differentiate from pampas grass, especially when immature.

Deschampsia caespitosa (Tufted Hair Grass). Forming a 3-foot, finely textured, tufted mound, this hair grass is useful either in sun or shade, in moist soil or dry. The leaves are evergreen and effective all winter long. Feathery, whitish green flowers are produced from late June through August, which is early for most grasses. Hardy to zone 5.

Elymus arenarius (Blue Lyme Grass). Silvery blue foliage is the distinctive feature of this coarse, invasive grass. Unless it is restrained, the persistent, creeping rhizomes can become quite a nuisance. It grows 2 to 4 feet tall and the leaves tend to grow in every direction, creating a jumbled, coarse appearance. Blue lyme grass will grow in nearly any soil, but is intolerant of shade. Hardy to zone 4.

Festuca ovina 'Glauca' (Dwarf Blue Fescue). This is a popular, small, tufted grass with finely textured, silvery blue evergreen foliage. It grows from 6 to 12 inches high in a neat mound. It must have well-drained soil, and prefers full sun or light shade. Frequent division is required as the center of the clump will die out, especially in moist, rich soil. Removing the flowers as they appear tends to prolong its useful life. In Southern California, festuca is one of the few gray plants that will do well with light shade, and its color is better without the browning at the tips sometimes caused by the sun. Hardy to zone 4.

Deschampsia caespitosa

Hakonechloa macra 'Alba-variegata'. This grass is a relatively recent introduction to U.S. horticulture from the mountains and forests of Japan. The long, deciduous, arching leaves are variegated creamy white. The plant spreads slowly by rhizomes, and is never invasive. Equally effective, in pots or planted in large drifts, the plant presents a neat, uniform appearance, reaching up to 12 inches high. Grow this grass in acid (pH 5.5 to 6.0) soil that has both excellent drainage and plenty of organic matter. Bright indirect light is best. Full sun is not recommended. The plant is hardy to at least zone 4.

Helictotrichon sempervirens, formerly *Avena sempervirens* (Blue Oat Grass). Resembling a large blue fescue, this tufted, mounded grass with bluish-green leaves reaches 2 to 3 feet high. The leaves are of fine texture. Plant it in any soil in full sun. In humid environments it is prone to fungal attack. The foliage browns slightly in winter. Hardy to zone 5.

Miscanthus sinensis (Eulalia Grass). Large, striking, upright and gracefully arching at the top, *Miscanthus* forms dense clumps 6 to 12 feet tall. The foliage is medium-fine in texture, turning a rich gold that is effective through the winter. The flowers, with their pinkish or silvery 7- to 10-inch plumes, are also attractive from fall into winter. The plant will perform well in any soil, and should have full sun. Hardy to zone 4.

'Gracillimus' is a finely textured cultivar with narrow, somewhat curly leaves. 'Variegatus' and 'Zebrinus' have foliage and stems in combinations of green with yellow or white. These cultivars are smaller than the species, rarely exceeding 6 or 7 feet in height.

Molinia caerulea 'Variegata' (Purple Moor Grass). This is a densely tufted, deciduous grass hardy to zone 5. The leaves are medium to fine in texture and longitudinally striped with creamy white. The flowers are purplish pink, up to 16 inches long, and appear in late summer and early fall. The plant ranges from 18 to 24 inches high and wide. This grass prefers acid to neutral soil, and full sun. It dislikes alkaline soil. It is native to open moorlands and heaths of Europe and Southwest and Northern Asia.

Pennisetum alopecuroides (Fountain Grass). One of the most graceful and popular of ornamental perennial grasses, fountain grass grows in a loose tuft 2 to 3½ feet high. From late August through October, coppery-tan flowers arch out from the mound like water spraying out of a fountain. In late fall the flowers shatter and the foliage turns yellow. Give it full sun and

Top left: *Festuca ovina* 'Glauca'
Top right: *Elymus arenarius* with *Lychnis flos-jovis* in foreground
Above: *Hakonechloa macra* 'Alba-variegata'

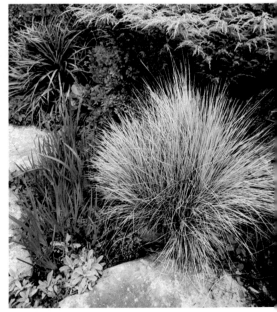

a fertile soil, and enough room to develop its 3- to 4-foot mature diameter. It is native to open ground and steppes of Asia, and is hardy to zone 5.

Left: *Elymus arenarius* (left), *Miscanthus sinensis* 'Gracillimus' (center), and Staghorn Sumac (right)
Above: *Helictotrichon sempervirens*

Schizachyrium scoparium, formerly *Adropogon scoparius* (Little Bluestem). This native of the eastern United States and Canada is useful either for naturalizing or in the border. Growing from 1½ to 4 feet tall, it presents a stiffly upright form with finely textured, bluish-green leaves that turn bronze or reddish and remain attractive all winter. The fluffy, small white flowers and seeds are effective from July into winter. It will grow in nearly any soil, but prefers those that are well drained and dry. Give it full sun. A striking blue selection has recently become available, sold wholesale out of Nebraska. Hardy to zone 4.

Gypsophila paniculata (Baby's Breath). Pink family. Native from Central and Eastern Europe to Central Africa.

Gypsophila's cloudlike mists of tiny white or pink flowers are a familiar sight in the perennial garden. Use it as a complement to bold-textured plants, or as a focal point in the border.

The flowers are usually white, but some varieties are pink or have a pinkish cast. The individual blossoms are tiny, either single or double, and are produced in massive quantities on slender, multibranched stems. The effect is airy and delicate. It blooms in July, but this can be prolonged into September by shearing spent flowers.

Gypsophila paniculata

The smooth, grayish green leaves are rarely noticeable below the drifts of flowers. The many stems are covered to the ground with blossoms, making the overall shape rounded and fluffy. Baby's breath reaches 3 feet high and as wide, often even wider. The plant is long-lived in a favorable location, and is never invasive. It forms thick, dense, fleshy roots.

How to Start: Easy from seed sown outdoors in spring or early summer, if the species is desired. Or sow indoors in spring at 60° to 70°. Named cultivars, often superior, are generally grafted onto the species rootstock. These should be purchased and planted in early spring. Be sure to set the grafted varieties with the graft union 1 inch below the soil level.

Where to Plant: The soil must be well drained and alkaline, and preferably low in fertility. Soggy soil, especially in winter, is usually fatal. Rock garden conditions are ideal. Give it full sun. Space plants 24 to 30 inches apart. Hardy to zone 3.

Care: Moderately easy. The plant is difficult to stake, and large cultivars and

Helenium 'Sunny Boy'

vigorous plants will need support to keep them from flopping and spreading open. The best method is to place a wire basket about 15 to 18 inches high and wide over young plants for the stems to grow through. In acid soils apply lime yearly, but do not let it come into direct contact with the fleshy roots. To prolong bloom, keep flowers sheared before they set seed. Once established, it needs little attention.

Although the plant is usually free of pests and disease, leaf hoppers and aster yellows have been reported. North of zone 6, mulching over the winter to protect from cold is advised; however, do not cover the crown until after the ground is completely frozen, or rotting is likely.

The thick, fleshy roots are difficult to divide, and plants resent the disturbance of transplanting. Division is discouraged, but if undertaken should be done in spring.

Related Species and Varieties: 'Bristol Fairy' is the most common cultivar, with excellent double white flowers on 4-foot plants.

'Pink Fairy' is a small, restrained plant growing only 18 inches high. It has a long bloom season, producing pink double flowers from July to frost.

Gypsophila repens is a low-growing species from 6 to 18 inches high that spreads widely by creeping, rooting stems. It is good in the front of the border, in the rock garden, or trailing down walls. One of the most popular varieties is a pink form, 'Rosy Veil'.

Helenium autumnale (Sneezeweed). Daisy family. Native to most of continental North America.

Sneezeweed is an unfortunate name for this plant, as it neither causes sneezing nor is it a weed in the garden. The small, daisylike flowers, despite their massive quantity, present a delicate appearance in the garden, as the rays of each flower head point gracefully back toward the stem. It is a relative of the sunflower and the black-eyed Susan.

Flowers occur in shades of red, orange, or yellow, with solid or bicolored "petals," or rays. The flowers are 1 or 2 inches across and appear at the ends of branched stems. They bloom in late July through frost.

The medium to dark green leaves are linear, up to 6 inches long, and larger and more numerous at the base of the plant. The stems are erect, then arch and spread at the top, making the plant wider at the top than at the base. Helenium can grow from 30 inches to 6 feet tall, depending upon cultivar and growing conditions.

These are vigorous plants and will rapidly overcrowd if not divided regularly. Grown properly, they are long-lived and seldom invasive.

How to Start: The cultivars, which are usually hybrid, will not breed true from seed. But the species can be sown indoors in early spring at 60° to germinate in 1 week. Purchased plants are usually grown from stem cuttings or divisions, and are best planted in early spring.

Where to plant: Best in soil of only average fertility that is high in moisture and organic matter. They are tolerant of many poor soils, however, including heavy, wet clay. Give them full sun. Space plants 18 to 24 inches apart. Hardy to zone 3.

Care: Moderately easy. The taller varieties need staking. Pinch growing tips regularly until mid-June to promote heavier flowering and bushy, dense growth. Sneezeweeds have few serious problems, although rust and leaf spot have been reported. Division should be performed every other year to prevent overcrowding. Vigorous plants may need annual division, but slower-growing hybrids may go as long as 4 years without it.

Helianthus decapetalus **var.** *multiflorus* (Thinleaf Sunflower). Daisy family. Native from Maine to Georgia, and west to Illinois and Minnesota.

This large, bushy sunflower produces great quantities of yellow or gold flowers in late summer. The blooms resemble dahlias, and are excellent in the border and for cut flowers.

The blossoms may be either single or double and are 3 to 4 inches in diameter. They appear in clusters at the ends of branched stems, blooming from August until frost.

Unlike many other sunflowers, the foliage usually stays attractive all season long. The large, oval leaves are a dark, dull green. The leafy stems are erect and somewhat spreading toward the top, where they become increasingly branched. Most varieties reach 4 to 5 feet high.

The plant forms swollen, fleshy roots similar to tubers. It is long-lived, restrained in growth, and never invasive.

Helianthus 'Italian White'

How to Start: It is best to purchase named cultivars from the nursery, or to divide selected plants in spring, as seed results in many inferior plants.

Where to Plant: These sunflowers are native to moist woods and bottom meadows, and so prefer moist, well-drained soil high in organic matter. Although full sun is best, partial shade is tolerated. Good air circulation is a distinct advantage. Space plants 18 to 24 inches apart. Hardy to zone 3.

Care: Easy. The tallest varieties may require staking. Water adequately and feed occasionally. It has few serious pests, although mildew can be a problem in moist locations with poor air circulation. Protect plants with fungicide. Division is the best means of increase, but is seldom needed for rejuvenation. Divide in early spring.

Heliopsis helianthoides **subspecies** *scabra* (Heliopsis Oxeye). Daisy family. Native to eastern North America.

The yellow or gold flowers of heliopsis are produced in incredible abundance over a long season. For its bright, solid color and length of bloom, it is nearly indispensable in the mixed border.

The flowers may be single or semidouble, but most cultivars are fully double. Resembling zinnias, they are 3 to 4 inches across and appear at the ends of long, branched, leafy stems. They bloom from early July to frost.

The dark green leaves are lush, dense, and lance-shaped or oblong to 5 inches in length. The plant is erect to spreading, bushy, and widest at the top. It grows 3 to 4 feet high. Always restrained in growth and never invasive, it is long-lived when divided periodically.

Heliopsis helianthoides subspecies *scabra*

How to Start: Best to divide named cultivars in fall or spring, or to plant nursery plants. Plants may vary considerably when started from seed.

Where to Plant: Best in moist, well-drained soil of average to moderately high fertility and high in organic matter. Give it full sun. Space plants 24 inches apart. Hardy to zone 3.

Care: Moderately easy. Water abundantly, especially during drought. Fertilize regularly. Aphids are the chief pest problem, especially on plants grown in poor soil. Otherwise, there are no serious pests. Rejuvenate by dividing every 3 or 4 years. Division is also the best means of increase.

Helleborus niger (Christmas Rose). Buttercup family. Native to Europe. Not even remotely related to the rose, this is an evergreen perennial that blooms in winter with large white flowers, often flushed with pale pink. It is useful in shady woodland spots under the canopy of deciduous trees.

The flowers are produced at the ends of several clustered stems. They have five showy sepals, 2 to 4 inches across, surrounding a center of attractive yellow stamens. They can bloom as early as November or as late as March or April, although the latter is more common. Winter bloom depends upon warm spells that thaw the soil.

The foliage appears to grow directly out of the soil without stems. The large, smooth, deep green leaves are compound, divided into seven or more leaflets, and are evergreen in zone 6 and south.

The clumps of foliage expand slowly by rhizomatous roots. The plant grows to 15 inches high and is long-lived, restrained in growth, and never invasive.

How to Start: Best started from nursery plants or divisions planted in spring. It can be started from seed, but this takes considerable time to result in plants large enough to transplant. Young (first-year) self-sown seedlings collected from around established plants are easy to transplant.

Where to Plant: Well-drained, moist soil high in organic matter and preferably acid or neutral (pH 6.5 to 7.0). The plant requires shade in summer and partial sun in winter, such as is found under the boughs of deciduous trees or shrubs (but try to avoid competing, greedy roots). Hardy to zone 3.

Helleborus niger

Care: Moderately difficult, being choosy about location. Keep evenly moist and never allow it to dry out. Mulch well with organic matter in summer and irrigate regularly, especially during drought. If the soil is extremely acid, apply lime yearly, but avoid letting it contact the roots, which are sensitive. Fertilize rarely, if ever, as the roots are easily damaged by nitrogen.

Leaf spot is occasionally troublesome, but easy to treat with fungicide.

Christmas rose resents disturbance of any kind, and never needs division for rejuvenation. Dividing for increase is possible but difficult. Any attempt to divide it should be undertaken in early spring after blooming is complete. Carefully separate the roots, ensuring that each portion has several roots and "eyes" (developing leaf buds). Set the roots so that the eyes are about an inch below soil level.

Related Species and Varieties: *Helleborus lividus* subspecies *corsicus* has apple-green blossoms in large clusters in early spring. This is the best helleborus for the mild-climate regions of the Southwest. Although reportedly hardy to zone 6, in the northern limits of its range it should be well protected from cold, drying winds in the winter.

H. orientalis (Lenten Rose) blooms from March into May. Varieties are available with flowers in colors from chocolate and purplish green to pink and white. The foliage is a lighter green than the Christmas rose, but the structure and cultural needs are nearly the same. It is hardy to zone 5 and is reported to be the best helleborus for the Southeast.

Left: *Hemerocallis* hybrids
Below, in descending order: *Hemerocallis* hybrids 'Just Mary', 'George Cunningham', 'Northbrook Star', 'Finest Hour'

Hemerocallis **species** (Daylily). Lily family. Most garden plants of hybrid origin with parents native to Japan.

Daylilies are very easy, long-lasting perennials with attractive foliage and showy flowers. The individual blossoms last only a day, but each plant continually produces new ones over a long season.

Daylilies come in many colors, with flowers in shades of cream, yellow, orange, red, pink, and violet; often striped and bicolored. Individually they are from 3 to 5 inches long, and open just as wide. They appear at the ends of long stems. Some cultivars are deliciously fragrant.

Flowering generally lasts 3 to 4 weeks, but this varies according to the cultivar. The bloom season is commonly divided into *early* (late May and June), *middle* (July), and *late* (August into September), although considerable overlapping occurs.

The bright green, handsome, straplike leaves grow 1 to 2 feet long, and are effective all season. The leaves arch out from the base of the plant, forming a mound of foliage. Stems and flowers arise from this mound.

Depending upon cultivar, daylilies can reach from 20 inches to 3 or 4 feet tall, including flowers. They all form a tough, heavy, tuberous root system. Some cultivars are evergreen in mild climates (zone 8 and south).

Daylilies are exceedingly long-lived and clumps will expand indefinitely. They are restrained in growth, permanent, not invasive, and compete well with roots of trees and shrubs. Most hybrids will not reseed.

How to Start: Nursery stock or division in spring or late summer. Sowing seed is a complex and intriguing undertaking for those gardeners interested in selecting and breeding.

Where to Plant: Daylilies are highly adaptable, but perform best in well-drained soil high in organic matter and of only average fertility. Tolerating shade or sun well, they seem to prefer full sun in northern areas, and partial shade in the hot South. However, delicate colors tend to fade quickly in full sun. Too rich a soil leads to the rapid growth of lush foliage and few flowers. Space plants 18 to 36 inches apart. Hardy to zone 3.

Heuchera sanguina

Care: Very easy. Water through dry periods and give an occasional light feeding. To improve appearance, remove the flower stalks after their blossoms are spent. The plant has no serious pests. Although most cultivars can be left alone permanently, some of the more vigorous ones give improved performance with division every 6 or 7 years. Division of mature plants is an arduous task due to the heavy root system, but it is still the best means of increase. Divide in spring or late summer.

Varieties: Cultivars are too numerous to mention here. Extensive breeding has resulted in thousands. Select plants for the features you want from descriptions in specialty grower catalogs.

Heuchera sanguinea (Coral Bells). Saxifrage family. Native to New Mexico and Arizona, south to Mexico.

Airy clusters of tiny bell-shaped flowers top the long, delicate flower stalks of coral bells. They are effective in the front of borders or as a small-scale ground cover in either sun or partial shade, and are hardy far north of their natural range.

The flowers are pink, red, white, or chartreuse. They bloom in June and July, but flowering can be prolonged into September by removing faded flower stalks.

The attractive basal clumps of foliage are evergreen. The leaves are dark or bright green, rounded, and 2 to 4 inches across. Some varieties are marbled with bronze or silver, and take on a reddish cast in fall that lasts through the winter. The plant grows 10 to 24 inches high.

The clumps of foliage will expand gradually from the center by the growth of long, fleshy surface roots. Although coral bells produce great quantities of seed, some of which may germinate in the garden, they could never be considered invasive. They are long-lived.

How to Start: Nursery plants or division in spring are the most common methods of starting. Make sure that each thick stem has a few roots, and plant the crowns 1 inch below the soil level. Coral bells are also easy to start from leaf cuttings made in late fall. Each cutting needs a short section of leaf-stalk, in addition to an entire leaf, to root in sand. Seed sown outdoors in early spring will produce flowering plants the next year. Merely press the seed into the soil and do not cover, as it needs light to germinate. Or sow indoors in late winter or early spring at 50° to 60°. Germination takes about 20 days. Seed from hybrids will not breed true.

Where to Plant: Coral bells are quite adaptable, but perform best in well-drained soils rich in organic matter. They prefer full sun but do quite well in partial shade. Space plants 9 to 15 inches apart. Hardy to zone 3.

Care: Easy. Removing flower stalks before they can set seed and abundant watering over dry periods will prolong flowering. Owing to the shallow, fleshy roots, coral bells are prone to frost heave in winter; during warm spells and in spring, the crowns may have to be pushed back into the soil. A loose covering, such as evergreen boughs, may help alleviate this problem.

Root weevils and mealybugs can be problems, and protection with insecticide will help. Stem rot can be serious in heavy, wet soils and humid climates.

The plants probably will need rejuvenation by division every fifth or sixth year. When flowering is reduced and clumps have become woody, it is time to divide. Younger plants can be divided for increase, an excellent means of propagation that should be done in spring.

Hibiscus moscheutos (Rose Mallow). Mallow family. Native to the marshes of the eastern United States.

Besides making an effective background up to 8 feet tall and covered with large, bold leaves, the rose mallow produces huge, dramatic, plate-size flowers up to a foot across. Marginally hardy in northern regions, they are a most useful plant for gardens in the Southwest.

The flowers are red, pink, or white, often with contrasting blotches at the interior. The blooms are single, 8 to 12 inches wide, and appear toward the tops of the branched stems. The flowering season is mid-July to frost. Flowering peaks in August, after which the blossoms decrease in size.

The leaves are green on the upper surface, whitish on the lower, oval, and up to 8 inches long. The foliage is dense.

The plant is erect to slightly spreading and from 5 to 8 feet high. Despite this height, the leafy stems are sturdy and rarely require staking. While they may self-sow freely in moist soil, rose mallows are generally restrained in growth and not invasive. They will live a long time.

How to Start: Easy from seed. Soak the seeds in water until they drop to the bottom of the container, then sow outdoors in spring. Germination is very fast, usually within 3 or 4 days. The resulting plants usually will bloom the next year. Because there is considerable variation from seed, cultivars are best started from divisions in spring. Set the eyes (leaf buds) of the divisions 4 inches below soil level.

Where to Plant: Rose mallows reach maximum size and lushness in wet, soggy soil high in organic matter; but they also perform well in average, well-drained garden soil. Give them either full sun or partial shade. Space them 24 to 30 inches apart. Hardy to zone 6, they are an excellent choice for the southern garden.

Below: *Hibiscus moscheutos* 'Southern Belle'
Bottom: *Hosta sieboldiana*

Care: Easy. Water abundantly in dry soils. Regular feeding will result in larger, lusher plants. Although Japanese beetles are attracted to the blossoms, the peak flowering season usually follows the peak beetle season. Leaf spot, canker, rust, blight, aphids, white fly, and scale can all be problems, although rarely serious. If necessary, protect the plants with a regular insecticide and fungicide program.

Division is never required for rejuvenation, but is the best means to increase a favorite cultivar. Divide either in spring or fall.

Hosta sieboldiana (Blue-Leaf Plantain Lily). Lily family. Native to Japan.

Lush, bold foliage is the outstanding feature of this plant. The large, bluish, heart-shaped leaves fan out symmetrically from a central clump. It is an excellent choice for a bold statement in a problem shady spot.

The flowers are pale lilac to near white. They are like small lilies, 1½ inches long on short, erect stems, and occur in clusters of six to ten blossoms. Often hidden by the foliage, they bloom in July.

The foliage is bright green when first emerging and assumes an effective powdery blue cast as the season progresses. The leaves are huge, 10 to 15 inches long and nearly as broad, and somewhat wrinkled on the surface. They grow in a basal rosette, the clumps reaching 2½ feet high and up to 40 inches across. The bold texture of the foliage is effective all season long. White- and yellow-variegated cultivars are also available.

This long-lived plantain lily freely produces seed, which sometimes germinates, but it could never be called invasive. The variegated cultivars will not breed true from seed.

How to Start: Plant nursery plants or divisions of young plants in spring. It can be grown successfully from seed, but sizable plants take 3 years or more to develop and will exhibit considerable variation.

Where to Plant: Hosta tolerates a wide range of soils, but is best in well-drained, moist soil high in organic matter. Avoid wet, soggy soils. Either partial or deep shade is satisfactory. They normally flower less in deep shade, but with this species the flowers are nearly concealed anyway. Full sun is likely to burn the foliage. Space plants 30 to 36 inches apart. Hardy to zone 3.

Hosta 'Chartreuse'

Care: Easy. The plant needs little attention once established, but should be watered deeply and regularly during dry spells. Young plants may profit from a winter mulch, especially if planted in the fall.

Snails and slugs can be quite destructive; use bait for protection. Other chewing insects may also disfigure foliage. Crown rot can be a problem in wet winters if the soil is not well drained.

Hosta never requires division, and may last 30 years or more in the garden. To propagate, divide only young plants up to 3 years of age, as older plants develop a tough crown that is hard to separate and even more difficult to establish.

Related Species: There are many species of hosta, ranging in leaf size from a diminutive 2 to 3 inches to the giant described above. Many have showy, sometimes fragrant flowers that add interest to the shady border, and some have variegated cultivars with white or yellow markings.

Hosta decorata (Blunt-Leaf Plantain Lily) produces 6-inch leaves rimmed with silvery white on compact, 2-foot plants. The flowers are a rich, dark violet, and are showy in August.

H. fortunei (Tall-Cluster Plantain Lily) produces many stems bearing showy clusters of small white or pale lavender flowers in August. The oval, light green leaves are 5 to 8 inches long. There are variegated cultivars.

H. lancifolia (Narrow-Leaf Plantain Lily) has slender, 6-inch dark green leaves. It produces great quantities of flower stalks bearing large clusters (up to thirty flowers each) of pale lilac flowers in August.

H. plantaginea (Fragrant Plantain Lily) is a popular old-time favorite with large, 4- to 5-inch fragrant white flowers produced in clusters from mid-August into September. The large, heart-shaped leaves, up to 10 inches long, are light green and form a mound that can spread to 3 feet.

H. tardiflora (Autumn Plantain Lily) produces large clusters of deep purple flowers just above the leaves. It blooms very late in the season, in October. The plants are small, to 12 inches high and wide, with dainty, dark green narrow leaves 4 to 6 inches long.

H. undulata (Wavy-Leaf Plantain Lily) has both fascinating foliage and very showy flowers, with the added advantage of being more tolerant of full sun than any other hosta. The leaves have a wavy margin, are striped with white and green, and are relatively small, 6 to 8 inches long. The pale violet flowers are generously produced on stems from 10 to 30 inches tall, and are quite showy in July.

H. ventricosa (Blue Plantain Lily) bears striking blue to deep violet flowers 2 inches long, generously arranged in clusters made up of 10 to 15 flowers. It blooms in July and August. The leaves grow up to 9 inches long and are oval with a delicate twist at the tip.

Iris **species** (Bearded Iris). Iris family. Most commonly grown cultivars are of uncertain hybrid parentage, with parents native around the world, mostly in the north temperate zones.

Complex hybridization has resulted in a monumental number of iris cultivars to choose from. All have gray-green, swordlike leaves, and their large flowers are available in every color and color combination imaginable. Height ranges from dwarf bearded miniatures 4 to 6 inches tall to the stately, tall plants reaching 4 feet or more.

The three outer sepals of each flower are called "falls," and have a fuzzy central portion called a "beard." The three inner petals are called "standards," and are usually erect and arching. The edges of the flower parts are often ruffled or laced.

The vast range of colors and color combinations have resulted in a specialized terminology for the plant. Generally, the flowers are divided into five categories:

1. A *self* is a flower with solid, uniform color.
2. A *plicata* is generally white or yellow, with contrasting "freckles," or mottling.
3. A *bicolor* has standards of one color and falls of another, usually darker color. Bicolors have several subclasses, including: *amoenas*, which have white standards and colored falls; *reverse amoenas*, with white falls and colored standards; and *variegatas*, which have yellow standards and falls of purple, red, or brown.
4. A *bitone* has standards of one color, and falls of a different value of the same color.
5. A *blend*, the last category, is a variety with two or more colors variously intergraded in the same flower parts.

Bearded irises usually bloom for 2 to 3 weeks in April, May, or June, depending upon the variety.

The gray-green leaves are held stiffly erect in a fanlike pattern. Tall stems arise from the foliage, branching toward the top to produce blooms on short pedicels.

The plants spread by rhizomes, producing large, indefinitely expanding clumps that tend to decline and die out in the center unless periodically divided. Each plant "rests" for a few weeks after flowering, during which time excessive feeding may be detrimental. The leaf tips tend to brown in the summer after blooming, especially in dry years.

How to Start: Nursery stock or division of rhizomes are the preferred methods. Dividing should be done after flowering is complete, but not later than mid-August. The rhizomes should be separated so that each division has one fan of leaves and several feeder roots. Set the rhizome so that the top is 1 inch below the soil surface, and the newest leaves (and main direction of growth) face the direction in which you want the plant to grow. Cut the leaves back to 6 inches after planting. Sowing seed is a complex and intriguing undertaking for those gardeners interested in selecting and breeding.

Where to Plant: Bearded irises must have well-drained soil, preferably of neutral pH, fertile, and fairly high in organic matter. Give them full sun for the best flowering. Space plants 12 to 15 inches apart. Hardy to zone 3.

Care: Moderately difficult. Water adequately but never allow the soil to remain soggy. Tall bearded rises are heavy feeders; feed once heavily in the early spring, and again at about half the strength 4 or 5 weeks after flowering has finished. Remove all spent flowers or developing seed pods regularly.

Top: *Iris* 'Dazzling Gold' (bearded hybrid)
Middle: *Iris* 'Graphic Arts' (bearded hybrid)
Above: *Iris* 'Broadway' (bearded hybrid)

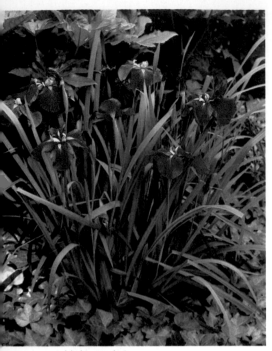
Iris kaempferi

Iris borer is a serious pest, inflicting severe damage and providing entrance for bacterial soft rot. Begin an insecticide program in spring when leaves are 2 to 3 inches tall, and repeat weekly for the next 2 to 3 weeks. Infected rhizomes should be removed and destroyed. Remove old foliage and litter in the fall as it may harbor borer eggs. The presence of borers can often be spotted by attentive gardeners before damage is noticeable. Watch for the trails of slime they leave along the leaf edge before tunneling down through the central portion of a fan into the rhizome.

Plants should be divided every third or fourth year for rejuvenation. Division is also the best means of increase, and is best done just after flowering is complete, when the plant enjoys a brief dormancy. It can also be done in early spring, but this may delay flowering until the following year.

Cultivars: Several hundred new cultivars are introduced each year, and available ones number in the thousands. Choose for color and flowering form from a specialist grower's catalog.

Iris kaempferi (Japanese Iris). Iris family. Native to Japan.

Massive, stately foliage and huge, flat blossoms distinguish this iris. It is quite finicky about location, but once established in moist, acid soil, needs little attention for a long, colorful life.

The flowers are white, blue, purple, lavender, and pink. They are often 6 inches or more across. The three overlapping outer falls (see page 111) are large, flat, and held horizontally, and the inner standards are small and spreading. It blooms in late June and July.

The dark green, swordlike leaves often grow 3 to 4 feet tall, and remain attractive all season. They are graceful, upright, and slightly arching in clusters topped by tall flowering stems. Stems usually grow 3 to 4 feet high, and heights of 6 feet are not uncommon in rich, boggy soil in mild climates.

Japanese irises are restrained in growth and long-lived. Their rhizomes gradually expand to form a clump.

How to Start: Nursery stock or division of rhizomes in spring are the accepted methods. Set the divisions 1 inch below the soil level.

Where to Plant: The soil must be acid, very moist, and well supplied with organic matter. The plants tolerate and even thrive in boggy or frequently flooded areas. Lime and alkaline soil are usually fatal. Give them either full sun or partial shade. Space plants 18 to 24 inches apart. Hardy to zone 4.

Care: Moderately easy. Water abundantly and maintain acid soil conditions. Feed occasionally with acid plant food. This plant has no serious pests. Rejuvenation is rarely needed; most plants can be left undisturbed indefinitely. Division is an excellent means of increase, however, and is best performed in spring, although it can be done in late summer after flowering.

Related Species and Hybrids: Many hybrids are available in white, reddish purple, rose, lavender, blue, violet, purple, and various combinations.

Iris pseudacorus (Yellow Water Flag Iris) is another large beardless iris that prefers very moist, acid conditions. The flowers are yellow and appear in great quantities atop 36- to 40-inch stems. This iris will self-sow prolifically in boggy, wet locations, and has become naturalized in many such areas in North America.

Iris, **Pacific Coast species** (Pacific Coast Iris). Iris family. Native to coastal western North America.

The Pacific Coast irises resemble small Siberian irises, to which they are closely related. They have delicate, open blossoms and handsome, grasslike, evergreen leaves. They are most suited to coastal gardens where the summers are mild, especially in the West, where they thrive in the wet winters and dry summers.

Iris 'Amaquita' (Pacific Coast hybrid)

The flowers are available in a wide range of colors from white to blue, violet, purple, rose, tangerine, orange, yellow, bronze, and brown, usually solid, but sometimes mottled. The falls (see page 111), which are frequently wider and more rounded than in the Siberian iris, are held horizontally, and in many cultivars are richly veined or blotched with a contrasting color. The standards, rather than being held vertically, open crisply at an angle. They bloom in late March or April in mild climates, or May in more northern areas.

The deep green, linear leaves are arched and rather relaxed in appearance. They are produced singly, rather than in a fan, and form solid, tight, grasslike clumps. They are evergreen and generally handsome all year long, although they may become browned at the tips toward the end of the summer dormancy period.

The plants have many branched flowering stems, which hold the flowers within or slightly above the foliage. Most varieties rarely exceed 12 to 18 inches high.

Pacific irises may occasionally reseed in optimum environments, but this is seldom a problem and they are never invasive. They hybridize freely, and extreme variation will result from plants grown from seed. Pacific irises spread by surface rhizomes, and their slow growth results in a gradual expansion of the clumps.

How to Start: Nursery stock or divisions are preferred. Division is best done in late summer or fall, but can be successful in spring just after flowering.

Where to Plant: Native to areas of mild, wet winters and temperate, dry summers, if planted in hot, wet-summer areas they must have perfect drainage and light shade to survive. They prefer well-drained soil high in organic matter and of only moderate fertility. In coastal climates, full sun is best. Space plants 10 to 18 inches apart. Hardy to zone 6, possibly southern zone 5.

Care: These irises require little attention. Fertilize only lightly in early spring. Remove spent flowers and developing seed pods. Do not water during the summer dormancy. The plants have no serious pests. Division is best performed in fall (September in the East, October or November in the West). It is rarely required for rejuvenation.

Iris sibirica (Siberian Iris). Iris family. Native to central Europe and Russia.
Exceptional hardiness, easy culture, long life, and durable, handsome foliage rank the Siberian irises as first rate for the border or landscape. All have nar-

Iris sibirica 'Sparkle'

row, linear, almost grasslike leaves of various heights, that support delicate flowers in June.

Shades of white, blue, and purple are the dominant flower colors now, but new hybridization work promises a much wider selection in the near future. The flowers are smaller and more delicate than those of the bearded irises. The three standards are erect, and the three falls are not bearded (see page 111). The blooms have an open quality and are borne in generous quantities on long stems that are somewhat branched toward the top.

The bright, dark green leaves can be as narrow as half an inch. They are clean and attractive all season long, and appear more relaxed than bearded iris foliage. Erect to arching clumps support many flower stems, with blossoms visible just above the leaves.

Depending upon variety, the Siberian irises range from 18 to 36 inches tall. The small rhizomes and deep tangled roots expand outward slowly to form dense clumps. The plants seldom need division, are not invasive, and can be very long-lived.

How to Start: Nursery stock and divisions. Spring is the recommended time for division and planting, although it is usually successful throughout the summer.

Where to Plant: The plants tolerate a wide range of soils, from extremely moist and rich to very poor and dry. They perform best, however, in moist, fertile soil of slight acidity. Give them full sun to partial shade; they will not flower well in deep shade. Space plants 18 to 24 inches apart. Hardy to zone 2.

Care: Easy. Provide abundant moisture and occasional feeding. To improve the plant's appearance, fastidious gardeners often remove spent flowers after blooming is complete. Although this plant is troubled by few pests, the iris borer can be a problem. Dig up any infected plants, cut out and destroy the infected portions, and replant the remainder.

Division is rarely necessary for rejuvenation, but occasionally an old clump will become too crowded and start dying out in the center. Division can be difficult, as the clumps develop quite deep and dense roots. It is an excellent means of increase, however. It is best done in spring, but can be successful up to late summer.

Related Species: Many hybrids of Siberian iris are available, mostly crosses between *Iris sanguinea* and *I. sibirica*. While too numerous to list here, the numbers are not nearly so overwhelming as with the bearded iris. *Iris spuria* is representative of a class of beardless Eurasian species, some of which grow 4 feet tall. Their rhizomes have a creeping habit and can spread quite widely; they rarely form dense, crowded clumps. The leaves are narrow, dark green, and handsome all season, except in hot, dry climates, where they die to the ground in midsummer. Many hybrids are continually being listed, ranging in size from 12 inches to 6 feet, and displaying a wide variety of flower colors in white, yellow, blue, violet, and bronze. Spuria iris are generally thought to be more tender than Siberians, and may need winter protection north of zone 6.

Kniphofia uvaria (Torch Lily; Red-Hot Poker; Tritoma). Lily family. Native to South Africa.

The torch lily produces gracefully arching mounds of grasslike leaves and rigid, erect spikes of brilliant flowers that lend an exotic, almost tropical effect to the garden.

The flowers are flaming red or red-orange, blending into yellow below. The species bloom in August and September, the hybrids in June, July, or August. The plant is hardy only to zone 7, but many hybrids have been developed that extend and soften the color range and also are much hardier, often to zone 5 if mulched in winter.

The medium- to gray-green foliage forms dense tufted mounds that either arch gracefully or, in some cultivars, are rigid. It is effective all season, and is evergreen in mild climates. The mounds are 12 to 30 inches high. From these arise the stiff, vertical "pokers," which can reach from 2 to 4 feet tall.

By producing young offshoots at the outer margins the clumps expand outward to about 3 to 3½ feet across in 4 to 5 years. The plant is long-lived.

How to Start: Best purchased as container-grown nursery plants and planted in early spring. Or plant divisions in early spring.

Where to Plant: The soil must be well drained; soggy conditions are usually fatal. Avoid windy spots, as taller spikes may get damaged or broken, and they are difficult to stake attractively. Give the plant full sun only. Space plants 18 inches apart.

Care: Easy. Mulch over winter where temperatures drop to 0° and below. There are no serious pests. Division may be needed every fourth or fifth year, but most clumps can go indefinitely without disturbance. Divide in early spring for increase. Either remove the young side growths individually, or dig the entire plant and divide the center clump.

Cultivars: Many are available in white, cream, yellow, gold, pink, coral red, orange, and scarlet. Among the hardiest are 'Earliest of All', coral rose in June; 'Springtime', coral-red and white; and 'Summer Sunshine', flame red.

Liatris spicata (Blazing Star; Gayfeather). Daisy family. Native to eastern North America.

Tall rose, lavender, or purple flower spikes make this plant a useful vertical accent for the garden. Use it either singly in the mixed border, or in groups of three or more.

The individual flowers resemble tiny thistle blooms and are packed densely along the 12 to 30 inches of the stems. Blooming in July to September, they open progressively from the top of the spike to the bottom.

The dark green, almost grasslike leaves are up to 16 inches long at the base of the plant and become smaller toward the top. They are stemless and arranged alternately along the flower stalk.

Blazing star can grow from 2 to 5 feet tall, although 3 feet is most usual in cultivation. Height varies widely depending upon growing conditions and heredity. The plant often self-sows but is seldom invasive. The clumps expand slowly by sending up new stems about the base. It is long-lived.

How to Start: The easiest method is to sow seeds outdoors in early spring or summer. Seeds must first be prechilled in the refrigerator for several weeks. Germination takes 15 days or more. Due to variability, named cultivars should be started by divisions made in spring, or from nursery plants.

Where to Plant: Native to wet meadows and marsh edges in eastern North America, this species responds to moist, well-drained soil high in organic matter and of moderate fertility. In wet locations it may self-sow prolifically. Give it full sun. Space plants 12 to 15 inches apart. Hardy to zone 3.

Care: Easy. Water abundantly. Removing spent flower spikes may produce a secondary bloom on lateral stems. When cutting a flowering stem, leave two-thirds for the plant's food production. It has few pests. In areas where the southern root knot nematode is known to be a problem, the plant should be avoided.

Crowded plants may require division every third or fourth year, but most can go many years without needing rejuvenation. For increase, divide in early spring.

Related Species and Cultivars: *Liatris spicata* 'Kobold' is an 18- to 24-inch dwarf with deep purple flowers.

L. scariosa (Tall Gayfeather) can grow from 18 inches to 5 feet high. It is

Top: *Kniphofia* 'Prince Igor' with *Verbascum* in background

Bottom: *Liatris spicata* with red *Monarda* in the background and *Heliopsis* in the foreground best known for its selections 'September Glory', a deep purple in color; and 'White Spires', in white. Both have tall flower spikes that open simultaneously instead of gradually from top to bottom. This species is native to sandy prairies and must have very well-drained soil that remains fairly dry over winter.

Ligularia dentata (Golden Groundsel). Daisy family. Native to China and Japan.

Large, bold leaves and tall spires of flowers make golden groundsel a useful specimen or border plant.

The small flowers are orange-yellow to bright yellow, about 2 inches across, and appear in large quantities held tightly against the tall flower stalks. They bloom in August.

The deep green leaves have a purplish tint. They are broad, rounded, somewhat heart-shaped, and grow up to 12 inches across. They are effective all season, but are prone to drooping and wilting in hot sun and during periods of high heat and humidity.

The plant forms dense basal clumps of leaves up to 18 inches high. From these arise 30- to 40-inch stiffly vertical flower stalks. Clumps expand at a moderate rate through the growth of short rhizomes. The plant is fairly restrained in growth and is long-lived.

How to Start: Divisions or nursery plants in spring are best.

Where to Plant: Moist, rich soil high in organic matter. Dry soils are quickly fatal, but the plant also resents sogginess. Partial shade is best, but it tolerates full sun, especially in cool climates and moist soil. Hot sun causes unsightly drooping of foliage, especially in humid weather. Space plants 24 inches apart. Hardy to zone 4.

Care: Moderately easy. Water abundantly. Feed regularly. Bait for slugs and snails. Division is rarely necessary, but is best performed in spring.

Limonium latifolium (Sea Lavender; Hardy Statice). Leadwort family. Native to Rumania, Bulgaria, and southern Russia.

Sea lavender's billowing masses of light, dainty flowers are often confused with a lavender or pink gypsophila (baby's breath). Its use is similar, for it effectively blends with and softens harsher forms and coarse foliage in the border. In its own right, it can also be attractive as a focal point.

The minute flowers are lavender or pink. They are produced in fleecy, cloudlike clusters on multibranched stems. The effect is misty and open. Flowering time is July and August.

The deep green, leathery leaves grow in basal rosettes. Up to 10 inches long, the leaves are semievergreen, and persist through the winter. The rosettes are often hidden by the mass of stems and clouds of flowers. The stems grow from 18 to 30 inches high and often spread as wide into a vase shape. The clumps expand gradually by producing new basal rosettes next to the parent plant. The roots are deep, tough, and extensive.

Sea lavender may reseed, but it is seldom invasive. It is generally long-lived.

How to Start: Easiest to purchase young plants, either in containers or bare root, from the nursery. It starts easily from seed sown outdoors in the spring or in fall, but flowering plants may take 3 to 4 years to develop. Soak seeds first for several hours in tepid water. Divisions or root cuttings are difficult to start, but possible.

Where to Plant: Sea lavender is easy and long-lived in well-drained soil of only moderate fertility. Heavy clay soils and excessive fertility can lead to long, weak stems that require staking. Give it full sun. Space plants 18 to 24 inches apart. Hardy to zone 3.

Care: Easy. Fertilize lightly each year in the spring. Tall plants may require staking. It has no serious pests. The plant rarely requires division and can be left undisturbed indefinitely. Division in early spring can be done for increase, but should be done so carefully; the plant resents transplanting.

Linum perenne (Perennial Flax; Common Blue Flax). Flax family. Native to Europe.

As perennials go, this flax is quite short-lived. It will reseed prolifically, however, and its small, clear, sky blue flowers on wispy stems are an asset to any informal garden or naturalized spot.

The individual flowers are about 1 inch across and last only a day; but they are freely produced over a long season, blooming in June, July, and early August.

Flax lends an airy, light quality to the garden. The plants are upright to spreading in form, open, and multibranched. Foliage is rare or nonexistent on the lower parts of the stems. The grayish-green leaves are narrow, short, linear, and held tightly against the stems.

The plant can become quite invasive by reseeding and should probably be kept out of any garden where tidiness is important.

How to Start: Flax is easily started by sowing seed outdoors in spring or summer. If sown in very early spring, it often blooms the first year.

Where to Plant: Best in Mediterraneanlike climates with a light, well-drained soil. It will tolerate a wide range of soils, but in wet soil is less hardy. Reliably hardy to zone 6, it may survive dry winters as far north as zone 4. Space plants 8 to 12 inches apart.

Care: Moderately easy. It requires little attention beyond keeping volunteer seedlings under control. It is rarely bothered by pests, but grasshoppers and cutworms are occasional problems. Flax resents transplanting; division is never needed and rarely profitable. It should only be attempted in the spring or fall.

Lobelia cardinalis (Cardinal Flower). Lobelia family. Native to eastern North America.

The cardinal flower is a tall, stately plant with brilliant scarlet flowers in mid to late summer. It is a fine choice for moist, shady spots, especially in natural gardens.

The individual flowers are small and grow in a spike along the upper 6 or 8 inches of the stem. They are attractive to hummingbirds, and bloom in late July to September.

The medium or dark green leaves are oblong or lance-shaped, growing to 4 inches long. They are arranged oppositely or in whorls along the stalks. The tall, vertical stems grow 3 to 4 feet high, and are topped with the blazing red flowers. Unfortunately, the cardinal flower is short-lived. It will self-sow under optimum conditions, but this is difficult to rely on. It is seldom, if ever, invasive.

How to Start: It is easiest to plant nursery stock or sow seed outdoors in late fall. Or, in late fall divide and plant new shoots that form around the base of the plant.

Where to Plant: Native to wet soils along streams, in meadows, or in wooded bottomlands, cardinal flower is best in well-drained, sandy loam high in organic matter and kept evenly moist. While tolerant of full sun if soil is kept moist, it is best in shade or partial shade. Space plants 12 to 18 inches apart. Hardy to zone 2. It does not perform well in regions of mild winters.

Care: Moderately difficult. Keep the plant well watered. Remove faded flower stalks. Mulch in summer to retain moisture, and in winter to protect

Top: *Linum perenne*
Above: *Lobelia cardinalis*

Lupinus Russell Hybrids

the crowns. Although several insects and fungal diseases can attack the plant, they are seldom serious enough to warrant protection. The plant should be divided annually to perpetuate it. Lift the clump, then remove and reset the outside clusters of new basal growth. This is best done in the early fall.

Lupinus Russell Hybrids (Russell Lupines). Pea family. Hybrids of uncertain parentage.

These huge, spiky racemes of flowers, available in nearly every color and combination of colors, are unfortunately adapted only to cool-summer, humid climates. Where they can be grown, they are outstanding either in the mixed border or massed in beds all to themselves.

Many types of lupine are bicolored, and most are available only as mixes. Individually the flowers are pealike, and are arranged in tight whorls that encircle the stem, creating clusters that are 1 to 2 feet long. Lending a strong vertical effect to the garden, they bloom in June.

The dark green, compound leaves are from 2 to 6 inches across and radiate out like the palm of a hand. They are produced on 6- to 12-inch stalks. Dense with foliage and bushy at the base, each plant sends up several flowering spikes.

In favorable climates lupines will self-sow profusely, but the progeny usually revert back to blue or white flowers. Clumps tend to expand and crowd, necessitating division, if the plants live long enough. They are relatively short-lived, but can persist long in the garden—to the point of being invasive—due to reseeding.

How to Start: Easiest started from seed, but they do require hand-pollinated seed, which can be expensive. Nick the seed coats or soak the seeds for 24 hours prior to sowing. Sow outdoors in place in spring or late summer, or indoors 8 to 10 weeks prior to setting out in early spring. Indoors, they will germinate in 4 to 5 weeks with 75° night temperatures and 80° days. Move them outside carefully, as they resent transplanting. Sowing in peat pots is the best method. Applying an inoculant for nitrogen-fixing bacteria to wetted seeds reportedly results in a more robust seedling. The plants also can be started from nursery stock or by division.

Where to Plant: Best in climates with cool, mild summers and high humidity. They prefer a neutral, well-drained soil of only moderate fertility. Give them full sun or partial shade. Space plants 18 to 24 inches apart. Hardy to zone 3.

Care: Particular about climate; but otherwise easy. Remove spent flowers before they can set seed. Mulch to retain moisture and keep roots cool. Water over dry periods. A light mulch in areas of harsh winters can be helpful. A regular program of insecticide and fungicide will help protect the plant from powdery mildew, rust, aphids, and the four-lined plant bug. Division is rarely necessary as the plants are short-lived. For increase divide in early spring.

Lychnis chalcedonica (Maltese Cross). Pink family. Native to the northern Soviet Union.

The small flowers of this plant are curiously shaped like a cross. They are brilliant scarlet-orange and are gathered into dense, rounded clusters atop 2-foot vertical stems. Rose and white cultivars are also available.

The individual flowers are small and five-petaled. They bloom in June and July. Consistent removal of spent flowers will encourage a secondary bloom in August.

The dark green, slightly hairy leaves are held at right angles to the stems. Leaves at the base are longest, up to 4 or 5 inches, shrinking to 2 inches at the top. Dense clumps of straight, vertical stems 1 to 2 feet tall support the flower clusters.

Lychnis chalcedonia

Maltese cross will reseed, and can become an invasive nuisance. It is generally short-lived. If it lives long enough, the clump will expand gradually by sending up new shoots around the base; it can become overcrowded and need division.

How to Start: Best started from seed sown outdoors in spring, summer, or fall. It will flower the first year if started early indoors, germinating in 3 to 4 weeks at a temperature of 70°. Do not cover the seeds, as they respond to light. Seedlings are difficult to transplant, so start them in peat pots. The plant can also be started by nursery plants or by divisions made in spring or fall.

Where to Plant: Soil must be perfectly drained; wet soil in winter generally is fatal. Give it full sun. Space plants 12 to 15 inches apart. Hardy to zone 3.

Care: Moderately difficult. Remove spent flowers to encourage a longer bloom season and a secondary bloom in August. Leaf spot, root rot (particularly in winter-wet soil), rust, and smut can all be problems. A regular fungicide program would be helpful. Divide in spring or fall every third or fourth year, as the clumps become overcrowded.

Related Species and Hybrids: *Lychnis coronaria* (Rose Campion) is a biennial or short-lived perennial with brilliant magenta flowers produced singly on silvery gray stems and leaves. The plant has an open, stretchy feeling. Although short-lived, it will self-sow with tremendous vitality. Plant one in your garden and its progeny will be around forever.

Lychnis × *haageana* (Haage Campion), despite its hybrid origin, still reproduces well from seed. The flowers are the same scarlet orange, but are larger and appear singly at the ends of the stems.

Lysimachia clethroides

Lysimachia clethroides (Gooseneck Loosestrife). Primrose family. Native to China and Japan.

Vigorous and easy, these bushy, spreading perennials produce flower spikes shaped like a goose's neck. The leafy, dense clumps are effective as a low background, and the white flowers are an attractive addition to the late-summer border.

The individual flowers are minute and grouped in dense spikes 6 to 8 inches long. The spikes are conical, relaxed, and bent at the ends into a graceful, S-shaped curve. They bloom in July and August.

Lysimachia punctata

The medium green, slightly hairy leaves are of medium texture and turn an attractive bronze-yellow in the fall. The clumps of erect to slightly spreading stems have a bushy appearance and grow up to 3 feet high.

The plant spreads rapidly and can become invasive if not divided regularly. It is long-lived.

How to Start: The easiest method is sowing seed in early spring. You can also plant divisions made in spring, or nursery plants.

Where to Plant: Best in moist, rich soil high in organic matter. Drier soils are tolerated in partial shade. In moist soils give it full sun or partial shade. Space plants 15 to 24 inches apart. Hardy to zone 3.

Care: Easy. Water abundantly. Crown rot and white fly have been reported as problems. The plant can go for years before needing rejuvenation, but division is usually required every 2 to 4 years to restrain the size of the clump. It is best done in the spring.

Related Species: *Lysimachia nummularia* (Moneywort) is a low, creeping plant generally reserved as a ground cover. Entirely different in appearance from gooseneck loosestrife, it bears brilliant yellow flowers in June through August. Like its relative, it can be extremely invasive, especially in moist soils and around well-watered lawns. It is very well adapted to wet, boggy conditions and shade.

L. punctata (Yellow Loosestrife) produces long, 3-foot, vertical stems covered with whorls of yellow flowers in June and early July. It can be invasive unless restrained, but is a sturdy and reliable plant.

Lythrum salicaria (Purple Loosestrife). Loosestrife family. Native to Europe.

The purple loosestrife is an excellent example of the perils of common names, for it is unrelated to the previously described plant, gooseneck loosestrife, and is also considerably different in both its appearance and behavior.

Purple loosestrife is a tall, bushy plant that produces erect stems covered with bright flowers nearly all summer.

The flowers are pink, magenta, reddish purple, or deep purple. Individually they are about an inch across, and are produced densely along erect, 12- to 15-inch spikes. They bloom in July to September.

The medium green leaves are lance-shaped and 2 to 4 inches long. They are produced sparsely in whorls along the stems. The stems are strong, almost woody, multibranched, and erect, growing 3 to 5 feet tall. Flowers appear on the top 8 to 15 inches of the stems. The overall form is a vase shape.

Although the hybrid cultivars do not seem to be so rampant, the species will reseed abundantly in wet areas. It has naturalized in the eastern United States, frequently choking out large areas of vegetation in swampy areas or around bodies of water. These plants are long-lived, gradually expanding into large clumps by continually producing basal shoots.

How to Start: Easy to start by seed sown in spring or fall. Germination takes about 2 weeks. The cultivars, which are generally superior, should be started by nursery plants or divisions made in spring. Seed-grown plants will vary considerably.

Where to Plant: Although purple loosestrife is best adapted to moist, shady areas, it will perform perfectly well in ordinary garden soil and full sun. Space plants 24 inches apart. Hardy to zone 3.

Care: Easy. Water abundantly for the best effect. Removing faded blossoms will improve appearance, possibly extend the flowering season, and prevent self-sowing. The plant has no serious pests. It can go many years before requiring division for rejuvenation. Division is the best means of increase for cultivars. Divide either in spring or fall. Use a sharp knife, because the dense, woody roots can be difficult to separate.

Macleaya cordata (Plume Poppy). Poppy family. Native to China and Japan.

Few perennials enjoy the stature and bold texture of the plume poppy. With large, scalloped leaves, the plants are immense and topped with fluffy, airy pink plumes in late summer. They are best used either as a background or specimen in more informal gardens, where their tendency to spread rapidly is not a problem.

The flowers are ivory, changing to a creamy pink. The individual blossoms are tiny, but they are grouped atop the stems in open, large, delicate clusters, flowering in July and August.

The foliage is always dense, lush, and free of pests. The 8- to 10-inch leaves are bright green on the upper surface and silvery white on the lower. A light breeze will add an interesting accent by exposing the contrasting color of their undersides. The upright, vertical stems are often so branched that a mature clump has a bushy appearance. They generally grow 6 to 8 feet high, but can reach as much as 10 feet.

Plume poppy spreads rapidly through underground stems. It will eventually form a dense, grovelike clump. It tends to become invasive, especially in rich soil, and can be difficult to control unless restrained with an underground barrier.

How to Start: Easily started from seed sown outdoors in spring, from nursery plants or by divisions made in spring. Germination is quite erratic, however, and may take anywhere from 10 days to a year.

Where to Plant: Macleaya does best in well-drained soil of only average fertility, and full sun. In rich soil and shade it is more prone to invasiveness. Space plants 24 to 40 inches apart.

Care: Easy if the roots are restrained. Be sure to sink a sealed barrier of sheet metal, plastic, or concrete at least 2 feet deep, unless you desire an uncontrolled spread. The plant should be watered abundantly, but fertilizing can

Top: *Lythrum salicaria* 'Morden's Pink'
Above: *Macleaya cordata*

Mertensia virginica

result in rampant growth. It has no serious pests. Division should be performed every 3 or 4 years, or as soon as the clump gets overly large. It is best done in spring.

Mertensia virginica (Virginia Bluebells). Borage family. Native to the eastern United States.

The Virginia bluebells have drooping, bell-shaped flowers that appear in spring. The erect, leafy plants are most attractive in an informal or wild garden.

The outer portion of the petals is sky blue and the inner part pinkish or purplish. Each flower is about an inch long, and they are produced in clusters that hang gracefully at the ends of branching stems. They bloom in April and May.

The medium green leaves are produced both in basal rosettes and alternately along the leaves. Leaves are about 8 inches long at the base, becoming smaller as they ascend the stems. All foliage dies back and usually has disappeared by July.

The stems, which reach 12 to 24 inches high, are gracefully relaxed and curved at the tips. Overall, the plant is erect and slightly spreading. Long-lasting in suitable locations, Virginia bluebell is restrained in growth and not invasive, but will self-sow here and there.

How to Start: Easily started from seed sown outside in early spring or fall, from nursery plants, or from the division of dormant roots in early fall. When planting divisions, set the crowns 1 inch below the soil level.

Where to Plant: The plant prefers a cool, moist soil high in organic matter; and is partial to deep shade. It does best in cool-summer climates of northern latitudes. Space them 8 to 12 inches apart. Hardy to zone 3.

Care: Easy, in the right location. Mulching will help keep soil cool and moist in the summer and also provide a continual supply of decaying organic matter. Keep the soil evenly moist but never soggy. Do not remove the foliage when it starts to degenerate, but allow it to die down naturally, as with bulbs. Some fungal diseases have been reported, but the plant generally is little troubled by disease or pests. Division is seldom required other than for increase. It should always be done in early fall when roots are dormant.

Monarda didyma (Bee Balm; Oswego Tea). Mint family. Native to the eastern United States.

Bee balm's vigorous, bushy clusters of erect stems are topped with fluffy, dense flower heads in shades of pink, purple, white, or red. They will attract hummingbirds, bees, and butterflies to your garden.

The individual flowers are small and tubular, arranged in single or double whorls into the rounded flower heads. Reddish-colored cultivars are especially attractive to hummingbirds. The plant blooms in late June and into August.

The dark green, lance-shaped leaves are perpendicular to the square stem and opposite one another. Like other members of the mint family, they have a slightly crinkled texture and are aromatic when crushed. They are dense, lush, and remain attractive all season. The dense clumps of erect to slightly spreading stems grow 2 to 3 feet tall.

Bee balm spreads rapidly, and sometimes invasively, forming dense mats of fibrous, shallow roots. With age the stems become sparse, lanky, and tall, unless regularly divided.

How to Start: Named varieties are generally superior to the species, and are best started by nursery plants or divisions planted in spring. The species is easy to start from seed sown outdoors in spring or fall. Or sow indoors in early spring at 65°. Germination takes 1 to 2 weeks.

Where to Plant: Best in moist soil high in organic matter and of only average fertility. Give it full sun. In shady locations and rich soil it can become extremely vigorous and spread rampantly. Space 24 inches apart. Hardy to zone 4.

Care: Moderately easy. Water abundantly for best appearance, but withhold fertilizer to forestall rapid spreading. Bee balm has few serious pests. In crowded situations with poor air circulation, several fungus problems, such as powdery mildew and rust, may occur. Although many sources recommend spring division as best, with care bee balm may be moved successfully almost anytime. The clumps will need division every 3 to 4 years for containment and rejuvenation. This is also an excellent means of increase.

Cultivars: 'Cambridge Scarlet' has flaming scarlet flowers and is one of the best and most popular varieties. 'Croftway Pink' has soft, rosy-pink flowers that fade to lavender. Other frequently offered cultivars are 'Snow Queen', with white flowers, and 'Blue Stocking', with light purple flowers.

Nepeta × faassenii (Catmint). Mint family. Of hybrid origin; parents are native to the Middle East, Spain, and North Africa.

While not a flashy perennial, the silvery gray foliage, abundant violet-blue flowers, and neat, mounded habit of the catmint are valuable additions to the border.

In flower, catmint is subtle, muted, and airy. The flowers are particularly attractive to bees. Flowering peaks in late May to late July, but it continues to produce flowers sporadically until September. A full repeat flowering in the fall is possible if the foliage is cut back after the summer bloom.

The individual flowers are small and arranged in whorls 2 to 4 inches apart along the upper 12 inches of the stems.

The hairy, oval, inch-long leaves have a crinkled appearance and grow densely along the stems. When crushed, the leaves have an unpleasant odor. Catmint forms dense mounds of erect, many-branched stems spreading from 15 to 20 inches wide and 10 to 15 inches high. The foliage is attractive all season long, and makes an effective silvery accent.

This hybrid is sterile and will not self-sow, but in rich, moist soil the creeping underground stems can spread invasively. It is long-lived.

How to Start: Nursery plants, divisions, or rooted cuttings can be planted either in spring or fall.

Where to Plant: Well-drained, sandy loam and full sun to partial shade is best. Space plants 12 to 15 inches apart.

Care: Easy. Catmint responds to abundant water and an occasional feeding. After the first flowering period is over, cut the stems back by at least a third. This will encourage a low, dense habit and another full flowering in autumn. The plant has no serious pests. It will need division about every 3 years. This is best performed in spring or fall, and is an excellent means of increase.

Oenothera missourensis (Ozark Primrose). Evening Primrose family. Native from Missouri and Kansas to Texas.

The Ozark primrose produces large, yellow, cuplike flowers on sprawling, almost prostrate plants. *Oenothera* species that bloom in the evening are commonly called evening primroses; those that bloom in the daytime are called sundrops.

The flowers are a clear, bright yellow. Up to 5 inches wide, they are papery and delicate in texture, and are produced solitarily at the end of spreading or trailing stems. They are lightly fragrant, and bloom in June to late August.

The dark green, lance-shaped leaves grow to 4 inches long and may be

Top: *Monarda didyma* 'Granite Pink'
Middle: *Nepeta* species
Above: *Oenothera* species

either smooth or hairy. The plant can mound up to 12 inches high and spread nearly twice that distance.

The Ozark primrose is long-lived and restrained in growth; although the flowers do set many seeds and often self-sow, it is easy to control. New growth is slow to appear in the spring, so cultivate around the plant with care.

How to Start: Sow seed outdoors in late summer, fall, or early spring. Germination is fast, usually less than a week, and if sown in early spring, may bloom the first year. Transplant seedlings when small, for they quickly develop fleshy roots. Named cultivars can be started either by cuttings taken in late fall, or by division in fall or spring.

Where to Plant: The plant must have well-drained sandy soil, and responds to the addition of some organic matter. Winter sogginess is usually fatal. It prefers high fertility, but tolerates poor, dry soils. Give it full sun. Space plants 6 to 12 inches apart. Hardy to zone 4.

Care: Easy. Removing spent flowers will prolong the flowering season. It tolerates mild drought, but responds to watering over dry periods. It has no serious pests, but the fungal diseases leaf spot and rust have been reported. The plant needs division for rejuvenation every other year. An excellent means of increase, it is best done in early spring or early fall.

Related Species: *Oenothera tetragona* (Common Sundrop) produces great quantities of small, 1½ inch, lemon-yellow flowers from June to August. The spreading, bushy stems grow to 2 feet high. Although the species will self-sow to the point of becoming a nuisance, several cultivars more restrained in growth are available.

Paeonia **hybrids** (Herbaceous Peony). Peony family. The parentage of the many hybrids is uncertain, but most are native to Eurasia, a few to North America.

Incredibly long-lived, with huge, fragrant flowers available in a vast array of colors and forms, as well as glossy foliage that is attractive all season, the peony is considered by many to be indispensable for the border. Its neat, bushy shape and easy culture make it also a valuable addition to the landscape.

Flowers come in shades of pink, white, red, and yellow. They are large, 3 to 6 inches across, and sit atop long stems ideal for cutting. They bloom in May and June.

Paeonia 'Janice'

Five basic peony flower forms are recognized.

1. *Doubles* are fluffy, almost spheroid flowers in which the stamens have developed into fully petal-like structures.

2. *Semidoubles* are similar, but in these the stamens are not quite so fully developed.

3. The *Japanese* form is characterized by one or more rows of petals surrounding a mass of sterile stamens that provide a frilled center to the flower.

4. The *Anemone* form is similar to the Japanese except that the stamens have been transformed into narrow, petal-like parts.

5. *Singles* have one or more rows of petals that surround a mass of golden stamens.

The leaves are a deep, glossy green, deeply lobed, and medium in texture. The emerging young shoots are reddish and very attractive in spring; and the leaves occasionally develop crimson tints in the fall.

Many leafy shoots appear from a central clump of fleshy roots, creating a bushy, rounded shape that can grow to 3 feet tall. The clumps expand gradually to spread as wide. Peonies are long-lived, restrained in growth, and neat.

How to Start: From nursery plants or by divisions planted in August or September.

Where to Plant: Peonies need a deep, rich, well-drained loam generously amended with organic matter. Full sun is generally best, although light shade is tolerated well. The latter is probably best for pastel shades that will fade quickly in hot sun. Space plants 2 to 3 feet apart when massing, 3 to 4 feet apart as specimens. Hardy to zone 5. They do not perform well in sub-tropical regions of the Southwest and Southeast, since they require some winter cold.

Care: Usually easy. Water adequately, especially during dry spells. Feed annually in the spring, but never allow fresh manure or fast-acting nitrogen to directly contact the fleshy roots.

Bait for snails and slugs in the spring, as the emerging shoots are particularly vulnerable. Botrytis and phytophthora blights are the major problems. Practice good garden sanitation by removing and destroying the old foliage in the fall; and prevent water from standing on the foliage in the cool of the evening. Regular applications of fungicide during bud and bloom may help to prevent botrytis blight.

Division is best accomplished in late August or September. Lift the plants and, with a sharp knife, separate the fleshy roots into segments that each have three to five eyes (the reddish buds visible at the top of the roots). Plant the sections so that the eyes face up and are *exactly* 1 inch below the soil surface.

Cultivars: Literally thousands are available. Check the catalog of a peony specialist for individual cultivar descriptions.

Papaver orientalis (Oriental Poppy). Poppy family. Native to Southwest Asia.

Oriental poppies produce large, crepe-paper-like flowers, and coarse, toothed foliage. They grow best in regions of cool summers, and are best used in conjunction with late-appearing plants that can take over in late summer.

Originally, scarlet-orange was the only available color of oriental poppies; but now a wide variety of pinks, reds, oranges, and whites can be found. Most varieties have black splotches and black stamens in the center of the blossom. The flowers are from 4 to 10 inches across, and have a rumpled texture. They are borne singly at the ends of long, hairy stems. They bloom in June.

Papaver orientalis

The light green or grayish leaves are large and hairy. They are dense at the base of the plant, smaller and sparser higher up. The foliage dies down and disappears in July and August, but often reappears in September to persist over the winter. The foliage supports many flower stems that reach 2 to 4 feet high. The stems have a serpentine, curving quality.

Poppies are fairly long-lived as long as the soil is well drained. The clumps of foliage expand gradually and can reach 3 feet wide. They should be interplanted with other plants to compensate for the vacant spots left by the dying foliage.

How to Start: Nursery plants or divisions. Divisions should be planted from August to early September. Set the root crowns 3 inches below the soil level. Mulch lightly over the first winter but guard against suffocating the young crowns.

Where to Plant: The plant must have well-drained soil; wet crowns, particularly in winter, are usually fatal. Adding organic matter can be beneficial, but the soil should be only of average fertility. It performs best in regions of cool summers, and is short-lived in warm-winter climates. Give it full sun or partial shade. Space plants 15 to 20 inches apart. Hardy to zone 2.

Care: Moderately easy, with excellent drainage. A summer mulch will help keep the soil cool and the roots moist. Take care not to damage roots with cultivation in late summer after the foliage has died down. Plants with tall stems probably will require staking.

Avoid letting water stand on leaves and crowns on cool days or overnight, as this invites bacterial blight and downy mildew. Aphids may present a problem, as may the northern root-knot nematode.

Oriental poppies will require division every 4 or 5 years for rejuvenation. This is best done in August or early September.

Cultivars: Over sixty cultivars are commonly sold.

Penstemon hartwegii (Beardtongue). Snapdragon family. Native to Mexico.

Penstemons produce colorful, trumpetlike blossoms of rose, pink, lavender, or white that are vaguely similar to snapdragons or foxgloves. Members of the genus grow naturally from Oregon to Chile; thus, they are most suited to mild coastal and other humid climates with temperate winters. In cold areas they are treated as annuals.

The flowers are tubular and about 2 inches long. They are arranged in open spikes and nod on slender pedicels. They bloom in June and July.

The medium-green, lance-shaped, almost linear leaves are 2 to 4 inches long. The stems are vertical, branching at the base. The structure is like an open, loose-flowered and bushy snapdragon. The plants grow from 1 to 3 feet tall, depending upon variety.

Somewhat delicate in nature, beardtongue generally is not long-lived. It will self-sow in a favorable climate, but the seedlings will be quite variable.

How to Start: Nursery plants or by sowing hand-pollinated seeds outdoors in late summer. Seeds may be sown indoors in early spring at 65°. Germination usually takes less than a week. Division in spring is possible, but more difficult.

Where to Plant: The soil must be well-drained and gritty, and preferably on the acid side (pH 5.5 to 6.5). Full sun is best, but it tolerates light shade. Space plants 12 to 18 inches apart. Penstemon should be considered only for mild, coastal climates. Hardy to zone 7.

Care: Moderately difficult; the plant is particular about location. Do not overwater, but be sure to water adequately during droughts. To prevent seed formation, cut the stems after flowering. Do not overfertilize. Mulch

Penstemon hartwegii 'Evelyn'

over winter to protect from cold. The plant has no serious pests, although leaf spot and rust have been reported. Fungicide is an effective protection. While difficult to transplant, many cultivars will require division every other year to look their best. This should be done in early spring.

Phlox paniculata (Summer Phlox). Phlox family. Native to the eastern United States.

Massive color and stately appearance are the hallmarks of this perennial phlox. Equally characteristic is the need for spraying, staking, frequent watering and dividing, and weeding out self-sown seedlings. Despite the work in raising phlox successfully, many gardeners consider it indispensable for the border.

Flowers come in red, pink, salmon, magenta, purple, lavender, and white. They are like discs about 1 inch across and are gathered into conical or hemispherical flower heads 10 to 14 inches across. They usually bloom in July to early September, but this varies according to cultivar.

The dark green leaves are lance-shaped and about 3 to 5 inches long. The 2- to 4-foot-high stems are dense with foliage, each topped with a large flower head.

Phlox self-sows prolifically, but the seedlings of cultivars all revert to their original magenta. This is a relatively short-lived plant. It requires thinning out of old growth annually, and division every third year.

How to Start: Best results occur from nursery plants or divisions made in either spring or fall. Most cultivars purchased at nurseries are root cuttings. If started from seed, it should be sown in fall.

Where to Plant: The soil should be deep, moist, well-drained, high in organic matter, and very fertile. It is best to add superphosphate generously to the soil when planting. Full sun is best, although the plant tolerates partial shade. Provide a location with good air circulation, but avoid windy spots. Space plants 24 inches apart. Hardy to zone 3.

Care: Difficult for a presentable appearance. Water abundantly, especially during drought, but do so early in the day and preferably from below to avoid getting water on the foliage. Fertilize regularly. Removing the flower heads, snapping them off just below the last flower, will encourage the formation of lateral buds, hence more flowers; it will also discourage reseeding. The plant will require staking.

Powdery mildew and rust, in addition to red spider mites in hot, dry weather, are the worst problems. Spray with pesticide and fungicide every 10 days to 2 weeks throughout the season.

Divide every third year to rejuvenate, but replant only the healthiest outer shoots of the clump. This should be done in either spring or fall.

Related species: *Phlox subulata* (Moss Pink) is an entirely different plant in appearance and care. It is low and mat-forming with bright green, dense, needlelike, evergreen leaves. It can make an excellent ground cover or bed in full sun and light, sandy soil. In early spring (April) it is covered with flowers in shades of pink, white, red, or lavender. The hues are usually of electric intensity. Moss pink is also hardy to zone 3.

Platycodon grandiflorus (Balloon Flower). Harebell family. Native to eastern Asia.

The balloon flower is a long-lived and easy perennial whose bell-shaped blossoms resemble small inflated balloons when in bud.

Its flowers come in shades of blue (the usual color), white, and pink. They are 2 to 3 inches across, and appear at the ends of long stems in the upper part of the plant. They bloom in July and August, and often into early September.

Top: *Phlox paniculata*
Above: *Phlox subulata*

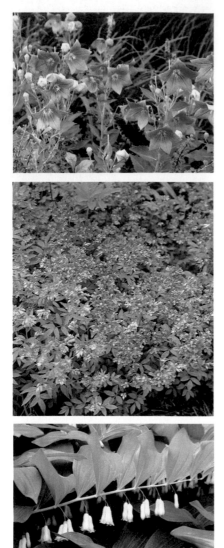

Top: *Platycodon grandiflorus* 'Mariesii'
Middle: *Polemonium caeruleum*
Above: *Polygonatum commutatum*

The leaves are medium green with a bluish cast to the underside. They are oval to lance-shaped, 1 to 3 inches long, and grow densely against the stems. The bushy clusters of erect stems are 2 to 3 feet tall. The flowers appear above and within the foliage.

Balloon flower is restrained in growth and long-lived. It is slow to appear in the spring, so be careful with early cultivation. It is also slow to achieve a mature clump; the full effect is seldom achieved before 3 years.

How to Start: The plant can be started from seed, but flowers will not appear for 2 to 3 years. Sow seeds in spring or late summer, and do not cover them with soil. Dividing gives faster results, but the plant can be difficult to transplant. Cut off the outer sections of the thick crown, retaining as many buds and roots as possible, and plant these divisions thickly to safeguard against some failures. Set the crowns so that they are barely covered with soil.

Where to Plant: Light, fluffy, sandy and well-drained soil is best. The plant tolerates many soils, but will not take wet soil in winter. Give it either full sun or partial shade. Space plants 12 to 18 inches apart. Hardy to zone 3.

Care: Easy. The plant responds to adequate watering, but will flower well in hot, dry locations. Removing faded flowers will extend the bloom season. Tall plants may require staking. The plant has no serious pests. Division is often difficult and usually gives erratic results. Fortunately the plants are long-lived and never require division for rejuvenation. Dividing for propagation is best done in spring.

Polemonium caeruleum (Jacob's Ladder). Phlox family. Native to Europe, Asia, and North America.

Useful mostly for its crisply textured, clean foliage in semishady locations, this perennial also produces mildly attractive blue flowers in the early summer.

The flowers are small, shaped like a cup, and grow to about ½ inch wide. Subtle in effect, they appear in loose clusters at the ends of erect stems. Flowering is in late May and early June.

The crisp, dark green leaves are compound and 3 to 5 inches long, with rows of 1-inch leaflets arranged regularly and opposite one another. They are fernlike in effect. The erect stems branch to give a mounded appearance, growing to 15 inches and spreading 15 to 20 inches wide.

Jacob's ladder is restrained in growth and relatively long-lived. It will self-sow, but seldom could be considered invasive.

How to Start: Division in late summer or seed sown outdoors in late fall or early spring are equally easy methods. Seeds can be sown indoors in early spring for earlier bloom: keep the germinating medium at 70° and sprouts should appear in 3 to 4 weeks.

Where to Plant: Any well-drained soil of average fertility. Light to partial shade is best. It tolerates full sun, but only cool climates. Hot sun results in unattractive, burned foliage. Space plants 15 to 18 inches apart. Hardy to zone 2.

Care: Easy in the right location. Provide extra water over dry spells. The plant has no serious pests, but leaf spot, powdery mildew, and rust can occasionally be troublesome. Division is seldom needed, but clumps will occasionally grow overly large and require it. Dividing is an excellent means of increase and should be performed in late summer.

Polygonatum commutatum (Great Solomon's Seal). Lily family. Native to eastern North America.

This subtle woodland native has long, attractive, arching stems and hanging clusters of tiny flowers. It is one of those rare plants that will thrive in dry shade.

The flowers are yellowish green to greenish white, about ½ inch long, bell-shaped, and droop in small clusters all along the undersides of the stems. They flower in May and early June.

Foliage is the chief attraction of this plant. The deep, rich green to bluish-green leaves grow up to 7 inches long. They are held perpendicular to the stem and alternate along its length. The stems, which are unbranched, often reach 3 to 4 feet in length. The plant spreads slowly by rhizomes, and can form broad patches in time. It is long-lived and not invasive.

How to Start: Nursery plants or divisions. Divisions should be planted in early spring or after flowering is complete.

Where to Plant: Great Solomon's seal is best grown in cool, moist soil well amended with organic matter. However, it will tolerate dry soil and intensive root competition quite well. Give it deep to partial shade. Space plants 18 to 36 inches apart. Hardy to zone 4.

Care: Easy to moderately easy. Water adequately and mulch over summer. It has no serious pests. Although never required for rejuvenation, division for increase is easy when performed in early spring.

Primula vulgaris (English Primrose). Primrose family. Native to Europe.

Primula is a complex and varied genus of several hundred species, varying in height from a few inches to as much as 3 feet. Most bloom in April or May in northern climates, and as early as February in mild ones.

In general, primulas form basal rosettes of attractive, often crinkly, and sometimes evergreen leaves. From the foliage arise vertical flower stalks bearing single flowers, heads, or umbels, sometimes arranged in tiers. The flowers in the genus occur in all colors.

Primula vulgaris and its hybrids are among the easiest to grow. This plant's flowers are pale yellow. Hybrids are available in a wide range of nearly every color except pure red and pure blue. The flowers are about 1 inch across, held one to a stalk just above the leaves. Prolific in bloom, a mature clump may produce more than a hundred flowers over a 2-month period.

The bright green leaves are tonguelike and produced in low basal rosettes, usually flat against the ground. They are evergreen where temperatures do not drop below 15°. Short flowering stalks grow from the center of the rosette.

Plants may go dormant in summer drought and re-emerge in autumn. They will self-sow in favorable environments, but are never invasive. Like most other primulas, this one spreads vegetatively, sending up new plantlets by way of surface roots near the crown. This primrose is fairly long-lived; however, frequent division is necessary to maintain vigor.

How to Start: Easily grown from nursery bedding plants or from seed sown in late winter or early spring on the surface of a moist, peaty soil mix. The seeds require light and humidity to germinate; so cover the flat with clear plastic. It is also easy to start from divisions made in spring after flowering is over, or in autumn.

Where to Plant: Although many species are quite hardy, primroses grow best in mild, humid climates that do not have extreme summer or winter temperatures. Most, including this species, should have rich, deep, moist, well-drained soil high in organic matter. Partial shade, preferably the shade of high tree branches, is best. Protection from hot afternoon sun is essential. Space plants 6 to 15 inches apart. Hardy to zone 5.

Care: Moderately easy. Although particular about location, this is one of the easiest primroses to grow. Water abundantly, especially during dry spells.

Below: *Primula vulgaris* Barnhaven hybrids

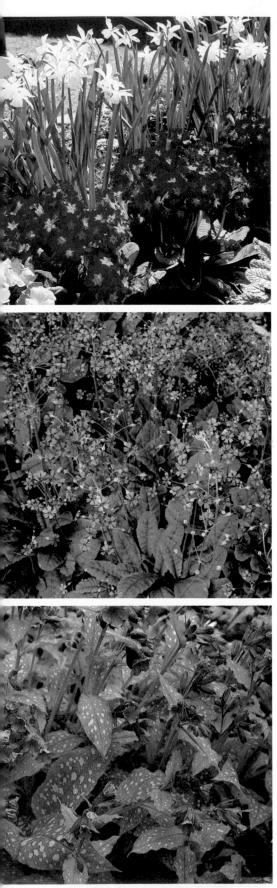

Adding organic matter yearly by mulching over winter should provide all the nutrition it needs. It has no serious pests if kept vigorous. Clumps should be divided every third year to maintain vigor. Divide after flowering in spring, or in the fall. Division is easy, and the plant quickly re-establishes itself.

Related Species: *Primula × polyantha* (Polyanthus Primrose) is the result of crosses made between *P. vulgaris* and several other species. This group is characterized by large, bold blooms, several to a stem, in a huge array of bright colors. Not as long-lived as *P. vulgaris*, they require essentially the same care. Division may be needed every other year, and occasional side-dressing with fertilizer is beneficial. In hot, dry weather, red spider mites can be a serious problem. Hardy to zone 5.

P. japonica (Japanese Primrose) is quite different in appearance, producing several tiers, or whorls, of magenta, pink, or white flowers along 2-foot stems. Like most of the candelabra types it requires a peaty, acid, and very moist or boggy soil, and can be difficult to grow if conditions are not exactly right. The blossoms begin to appear in May and often last through June. Other candelabra primroses are: *P. burmanica* and *P. beesiana*, both having purple flowers; *P. bulleyana* and *P. helodoxa*, yellow flowers; and *P. cockburniana* and *P.* 'Pagoda' hybrids, orange flowers. All Japanese primroses require similar culture.

P. sieboldii has bright green, wrinkled leaves with scalloped edges and clusters of lilac-pink flowers on 6- to 9-inch stems in late spring. Hybrids are available in many shades of white, pink, and purple, including bicolors.

Pulmonaria saccharata (Bethlehem Sage). Borage family. Native to Europe.

The Bethlehem sage's deep green leaves speckled with white make an attractive ground cover in the shade. Small flowers in early spring are a decided extra advantage, and it is easy to grow.

Flowers are blue, reddish violet, or white. Individually they are trumpet-like and about ½ inch long. They appear in relaxed clusters on stalks 10 to 12 inches tall. The flowers are often pink in bud, changing to blue as they open. They bloom in early April and May.

The exceedingly attractive, glossy leaves are oval to heart-shaped, and grow to about 6 inches long. The basal rosettes of leaves reach 6 or 8 inches high. From the crown arise several flowering stalks. The foliage remains attractive all season long.

The crowns gradually expand by producing more leaves at the outer edge of the clump. The plant is long-lived, restrained in growth, and not invasive.

How to Start: Nursery plants or by divisions planted in fall or very early spring. Water fall-planted divisions heavily until the ground freezes.

Where to Plant: Moist soil high in organic matter is best, although it need not be fertile. Give these plants partial to deep shade. Space them 10 inches apart. Hardy to zone 4.

Care: Easy. The plant requires little attention. Watering over dry spells is beneficial. It has no serious pests. While seldom required, division is an excellent means of increase. It is best done in late summer or very early spring, although success is common even during full bloom.

Related Species and Cultivars: *Pulmonaria saccharata* 'Mrs. Moon' is a form with larger flowers that are pink in bud and bright blue when open.

P. angustifolia (Blue Lungwort) has plain dark green leaves that are quite hairy, almost bristly. The flowers are showy, pink in bud opening to blue, and appear in April and May. Several cultivars are available, including pink, salmon, white, and red ones. These may be listed under *P. saccharata* in some sources.

Top: *Primula × polyantha* with white *Narcissus* and yellow *Primula vulgaris*

Middle: *Primula cockburniana*

Above: *Pulmonaria saccharata*

Rudbeckia fulgida 'Goldsturm' (Goldsturm Black-eyed Susan; Cone-flower). Daisy family. Native to eastern North America.

Unlike many other members of this genus, this is a true, long-lived perennial that is not the least bit weedy. The deep yellow daisies of this plant are produced in great quantities over a long season in late summer. This cultivar is probably the best for its profuse bloom and its even, 2½-foot growth.

The flowers are deep yellow with a black central cone. They are about 3 to 4 inches across, and nearly cover the plant over a long season, blooming from mid-July to mid-September. The cones persist and are attractive most of the winter.

The dark green, somewhat hairy leaves are lush and dense. The multi-branched stems are erect and spreading, usually growing to 30 inches tall. The overall form is a vase shape. The flowers are produced singly at the ends of the branches, often covering the foliage. Unlike most other rudbeckias, the foliage of this one remains clean and attractive all season.

Most black-eyed Susans are weedy self-sowers and are short-lived. This one is neither, having a restrained growth that will last for years in the garden. The clumps will expand gradually, sending up new shoots at the outer edges.

How to Start: Nursery plants or division in spring are best. Fall planting too is generally successful.

Where to Plant: Well-drained, moist soil of average fertility. The plant prefers full sun; in shade it will have an open habit and produce fewer flowers. Space 12 to 24 inches apart. Hardy to zone 4.

Care: Easy. Rudbeckia requires little attention and never needs staking. Water over dry periods. Aphids may be a problem, but are easily controlled with insecticide. Downy mildew, rust, and powdery mildew should be controlled with a fungicide. Division is best performed in spring, but is usually successful in fall as well. Most clumps will need dividing every fourth or fifth year to maintain their vigor.

Related Species and Cultivars: *Rudbeckia hirta* 'Gloriosa Daisy' is often sold as a perennial, although in nearly all cases it is short-lived and may behave as a self-sowing annual.

R. laciniata 'Goldquelle' is like *R. fulgida* 'Goldsturm', except slower growing and with double flowers.

Salvia × superba (Perennial Salvia). Mint family. Parents native to the Mediterranean region.

Spikes of violet-purple flowers and gray-green foliage that last throughout the season make this plant a welcome addition to the mixed border or individual beds.

The individual flowers are tiny and densely whorled around the spikes, which are 4 to 8 inches long. They bloom in June or August, and are surrounded by red-violet bracts that persist after the flowers are finished, providing a long, colorful season. The blooms are good for cut flowers and for drying for winter arrangements.

The leaves are of medium texture and effective all season long. They are aromatic when crushed. The multibranched stems are densely clothed in leaves, and the plant grows 2 to 3 feet tall.

Perennial salvia can be long-lived if conditions are favorable, especially if the soil is well drained. It stays in place and, since it is sterile, never self-sows.

How to Start: By nursery plants, or by stem cuttings or divisions planted in spring.

Rudbeckia fulgida 'Goldsturm' with *Pennisetum alopecuriodes*

Top: *Salvia × superba*
Above: *Scabiosa caucasica*

Where to Plant: The soil must be well-drained. Give it full sun. It will withstand heat, drought, and poor soil well. Wet soil in winter is usually fatal. Space plants 1 to 2 feet apart. An excellent choice for the southern states, it is hardy to zone 5, but success is frequent farther north with a mulch for winter protection.

Care: Easy in the right location. In northern zones apply a protective mulch after the soil freezes. Remove spent flowers to prolong the bloom period. Leaf spot, rust, scale, and white fly can be minor problems. Division is best done in spring. The root system is long and stringy, and re-establishment is usually slow. Fortunately, division is rarely required for rejuvenation.

Related Species and Varieties: *Salvia azurea* (Azure Sage) is a large, 4- to 5-foot plant with intense, gentian-blue flowers appearing in late summer and early fall. It is less hardy to zone 6. Variety *grandiflora*, often listed in catalogs as *S. pitcheri*, has more brilliant, deeper blue flowers.

S. pratensis (Meadow Clary), formerly *S. haematodes*, is a multibranched plant with many flowering stems in lavender blue arising above a basal clump of foliage. It blooms in June. Because it often behaves as a biennial, it is wise to set out new plants yearly to perpetuate it in the garden, so that new plants are coming on each year.

Scabiosa caucasica (Pincushion Flower). Teasel family. Native to the Caucasus.

The pincushion flower's pastel blue, sometimes white flowers on open, branching stems bloom nearly all summer long. It is seldom planted as a specimen, but it is an asset to the mixed, informal border.

The pale blue petals surround a hemisphere of protruding gray stamens that resemble pins in a pincushion. They bloom in June to September, growing to 3 inches across and appearing at the ends of the stems.

The medium green basal leaves are oblong to lance-shaped and measure up to 5 inches. The stem leaves are toothed and smaller. The foliage is large and dense at the base of the plant, becoming smaller and sparser on the stems. The stems are upright and arching, and grow in open and loose clusters.

With periodic division this is a relatively long-lived plant. It is restrained in habit. Clumps will expand gradually by sending up shoots at the outer perimeter.

How to Start: Sow purchased seed in early spring, or sow indoors at 65°. Germination takes 1 to 2 weeks. It may possibly bloom by the end of the first season. Or sow freshly collected, ripe seed outdoors in early fall. Scabiosa may also be started by nursery plants or by planting divisions in spring.

Where to Plant: Because summer drought and winter sogginess are both fatal, the plant requires the difficult-to-achieve combination of perfect drainage and moist soil. Sandy loam generously amended with organic matter is best. Give it full sun. Space plants 10 to 15 inches apart. Hardy to zone 2.

Care: Moderately easy. Mulch in summer and water over dry periods. Remove faded flowers to prolong the flowering period. Mulching over winter is recommended in harsh climates. There are few serious pests, but mildew and root rot have been reported. The clumps will start to degenerate in the third or fourth year, requiring division to restore vigor. This is also an excellent means of increase, and should be done in the spring.

Sedum spectabile (Showy Stonecrop; Showy Sedum). Stonecrop family. Native to China and Korea.

These mounded, 2-foot plants have fleshy, light green leaves topped with many flat clusters of flowers from August to frost. They are especially effective massed in a border, or in beds all to themselves.

The flowers are various shades of pink, rose, and white, turning to bronze as they mature and develop fruit in the fall. Individually, they are tiny and appear in dense, flat-topped or hemispherical clusters 3 to 4 inches across, often covering the top of the plant. Most cultivars are attractive to butterflies. They bloom in early August to the middle of September. The bronze fruits are attractive well into frost.

The light green leaves often appear dusted with white, and are thick, fleshy, and rounded. Growing to about 3 inches across, they are arranged either oppositely or whorled against the succulent stems.

Clusters of many upright to spreading stems are densely covered with leaves, each stem ending in a flat flower cluster. The overall form is mounded, neat and tidy, growing 18 to 24 inches high. The foliage is clean and attractive all season.

The clumps will expand by producing new shoots on the outer edges. In very rich soils they have a tendency to spread apart, revealing an open center. The showy sedum is a long-lived plant and is never invasive.

How to Start: Nursery plants and divisions are best planted in spring. Stem cuttings root easily and should be made in summer. Seeds can be sown in late summer or mid-spring at 65°. Cultivars will not breed true from seed.

Where to Plant: Sedums are not particular about soil as long as it is well drained. This group needs moist, richer soil than usually supposed for sedum and will grow in quite wet ones. Give the plants full sun, but partial shade is best in hot climates. Space plants 12 to 18 inches apart. Hardy to zone 3.

Care: Easy. This sedum responds to adequate water. It has no serious pests. Although the plant can go many years without requiring division for rejuvenation, it is an excellent means of increase and is best done in spring.

Sempervivum tectorum (Hens and Chickens). Stonecrop family. Native to Europe.

This curious low, fleshy perennial is grown chiefly for its dense rosettes of leaves. It is especially useful in dry, stony soil.

The flowers are purplish to red, about 1 inch across, and appear on surprisingly tall, hairy, curving to upright stalks 6 to 15 inches high. Although the plant is grown primarily for its foliage, the flowers are still interesting. They bloom in midsummer.

The leaves are usually bright green but some varieties have a red, purplish, or whitish cast. They are fleshy, as long as 3 or 4 inches on mature plants, and form a cluster resembling a green rose. Spined at the tips and evergreen, they often have a bronze or reddish cast in the winter. The rosettes, at most 4 inches high and 5 inches wide, rest snugly against the ground or nestle close to rocks.

The larger rosettes will produce many offspring from surface roots. Tightly clustered around their parent, in time a colony can spread into a dense, irregular, mounded carpet. The plant grows slowly, is not invasive, and is long-lived.

How to Start: Divisions or nursery plants can be planted successfully nearly anytime during the growing season, from spring to fall.

Where to Plant: Soil must be well drained. Avoid very moist, rich soils, and give the plants full sun. Space them 3 to 6 inches apart. Hardiness varies from zone 5 to zone 6, depending upon variety.

Care: Easy. Avoid overwatering. Rust and crown rot can be serious problems in damp locations and in soggy soil. Although seldom required for

Top: *Sedum* 'Autumn Joy' with *Yucca filamentosa* and *Calamagrostis epigeous* in rear

Above: *Sempervivum* species

Solidago canadensis 'Golden Baby'

rejuvenation, division is an excellent way to propagate sempervivum. Divide any time during the growing season.

Related Species and Cultivars: Sempervivums hybridize readily, and many forms are available, along with considerable confusion over names.

S. *arachnoideum* (Cobweb Hen-and-Chickens) has numerous white threads within and connecting the leaf tips that give it its appropriate common name.

Solidago **hybrids** (Goldenrod). Daisy family. While the parentage is uncertain, most are probably from Europe and the eastern United States.

Much successful hybridizing has resulted in outstanding golden yellow color on solid, easily grown plants.

Contrary to popular belief, goldenrod does not cause hay fever. The heavy, waxy pollen is insect-borne, and never travels on the wind. The insidious hay-fever-causing ragweeds (*Ambrosia* species) bloom at approximately the same time. No doubt this has led to blaming the more conspicuous, and innocent, goldenrod.

The flowers appear in various shades of yellow, from primrose and canary to dark gold. Individually they are tiny, but they are produced in great quantities in flat-topped clusters, or along pedicels held perpendicular to the stem. They bloom in August and September.

The medium green, lance-shaped leaves are held tightly against the upright stems. The branching, upright or slightly spreading stems grow in clusters, 18 to 40 inches tall and generally in a vase shape.

Goldenrods are long-lived, restrained in growth, and never invasive. They slowly increase by sending up shoots along the outside perimeter of the clump.

How to Start: Plant nursery plants or divisions either in spring or fall.

Where to Plant: Goldenrods are quite adaptable to most any soil, although very wet or dry ones should be avoided. Give them full sun. Space plants 12 to 15 inches apart. Hardy to zone 3.

Care: Easy. The tallest varieties may require staking if grown in rich soils. The plant has no serious pests. It can go for years without requiring division for rejuvenation. To increase, divide in spring or late fall.

Stachys byzantina (Lamb's Ear; Woolly Betony). Mint family. Native to Turkey and Southwest Asia.

Lamb's ear is a low, tufted plant grown for its outstanding foliage. The leaves are densely woolly and an intense, silvery white. It makes an eye-catching accent in the front of the border, particularly on moonlit nights. And it is especially pleasing when combined with pastel shades of blue and pink flowers.

The flowers of lamb's ear are purplish white. Individually they are small, about ½ inch long, and arranged in whorls at the top of 4- to 6-inch spikes. They bloom from July through September, and are pleasant but not particularly showy. The plant is grown primarily for its foliage. ('Silver Carpet' is a nonflowering form.)

The leaves grow to an oblong or tonguelike shape 4 to 6 inches long. They are arranged in low radial clumps 6 to 12 inches high and often spread 24 inches wide. Lamb's ear can be quite long-lived, but is always neat and restrained in its growth. The clumps expand slowly, but after several years they begin to die out in the center, necessitating division.

How to Start: Nursery plants or division in spring are the usual methods, but this plant is easy to start from seed sown outdoors in mid-spring, or indoors in early spring at 65°. Germination usually takes less than a week.

Left: *Stachys byzantina* with edging lobelia and *Achilles ptarmica* 'The Pearl'
Below: *Stachys officinalis*
Bottom: *Stokesia laevis*

Where to Plant: The soil must have perfect drainage, and should be of only moderate fertility. Lamb's ear is prone to rotting in muggy, humid climates. Give it full sun. Space plants 10 to 15 inches apart. Hardy to zone 4.

Care: Moderately easy. Avoid overwatering. There are no serious pests. Divide after the fourth year to rejuvenate. Division is also an excellent means of increase.

Related Species: *Stachys grandiflora* (Big Betony) is a taller, bushy plant with grayish-green leaves. It produces great quantities of bright purple flowers 1 inch long and gathered in whorls around tall spikes. It blooms in May and June. The flowers attract bees. The plant grows best in partial shade.

S. officinalis is similar to big betony, but with smaller, less impressive flowers. It produces tall, whorled flower spikes of rosy purple in July and August. It does best in full sun and a dry soil.

Stokesia laevis (Stokes' Aster). Daisy family. Native to South Carolina south to Louisiana and Florida.

The flowers of this perennial resemble a cross between an aster and a pincushion flower. They are most effective when grown in small groups in the mixed border.

The flowers are lavender to silvery or dark blue, and sometimes pure white. Like a daisy, they have an outer single or double row of "petals," or, more accurately, ray florets, and a center of fuzzy-looking disc florets in the same color. They are produced singly at the ends of the stems, blooming in July and August.

The narrow, dark green, lance-shaped leaves can grow to 8 inches long. Large basal clumps of leaves support many flower stalks. The plant grows 12 to 18 inches high. The Stokes' aster can be long-lived if the soil is perfectly drained in winter.

How to Start: The plant is easy to start from seed sown outdoors in April. Nursery plants or clump divisions can also be planted in the spring.

Where to Plant: Stokes' aster is definitely intolerant of wet soil in winter, so good drainage is a must. Otherwise it is not too particular about soil. Give it full sun. Space plants 12 to 15 inches apart. Hardy to zone 6.

Care: Moderately difficult, being quite particular about soggy soil in winter. Otherwise, it requires little special attention. There are no serious pests. Division is required about every 4 years to reduce crowding. Also a good means of increase, it is best performed in spring.

Thalictrum aquilegifolium with tulips

Thalictrum rochebrunianum (Lavender Mist Meadowrue). Buttercup family. Native to Japan.

These tall, airy plants have finely textured foliage topped with delicate sprays of lavender flowers. Growing 3 to 6 feet or more high, this meadowrue makes a splendid background.

The flowers are lavender-violet with bright yellow stamens. Individually they are minute and have no petals; the showy parts are the purplish sepals and yellow stamens. They appear in great quantities on open, misty panicles, blooming in July and August.

The very delicate, medium-green leaves often have a bluish cast. They are compound with many small three-leaf leaflets. The tall, multibranched stems grow 3 to 6 feet, and sometimes taller. An open, lacy appearance belies strong stems that never require staking. The foliage effect is similar to that of maidenhair fern, with which the plant is often compared.

Thalictrum grows slowly and is long-lived. New divisions may take two or three seasons to achieve the effect desired.

How to Start: Seeds should be sown outdoors in the fall. Fresh seed will germinate best. Seed can be sown in spring if given a 3- to 5-week period of prechilling in the refrigerator; but germination is often erratic. Nursery plants or divisions planted in spring are preferable, although fall plantings are usually successful with winter protection.

Where to Plant: The plant prefers deep, rich, moist soil high in organic matter. Partial shade is best, but full sun is tolerated if the soil is kept moist. Space plants 24 inches apart. Hardy to zone 5.

Care: Moderately easy. Meadowrue needs abundant water. It has few serious pests, but powdery mildew and rust occur occasionally. It is best to divide the plant about every fifth year to relieve crowding of the root mass. An excellent means of increase, this should be done either in spring or fall. Divisions planted in fall should be mulched over winter.

Thermopsis caroliniana (False Lupine). Pea family. Native from North Carolina to Georgia.

Resembling a tall, slender yellow lupine, with its spike of pealike flowers, thermopsis will withstand the hot, muggy weather of the Southeast. It is also easy and completely hardy elsewhere in the United States. It may be difficult to locate commercially, since it is relatively unknown.

The individual flowers are small and are gathered into 10- to 12-inch spikes on erect stems. They bloom in June and early July.

The dark green leaves are divided into three leaflets. The plant forms clusters of rigidly upright stems covered with leaves and tipped with flower spikes. It grows up to 4 feet tall and often spreads 3 feet wide.

False lupine is long-lived and restrained in growth. It seldom needs division. Early to appear and fast-growing in the spring, the foliage remains lush and dense all season long.

How to Start: Easy to start from seed sown in late summer. Before sowing, soak the seeds in warm water or file the seed coats. The plant can also be started with nursery plants or from clump divisions planted in late summer.

Where to Plant: Well-drained soil of poor to average fertility. Like most members of the pea family, root nodules "fix" nitrogen from the atmosphere; the false lupine almost never needs fertilizing, and soil that is excessively rich in nitrogen will promote yellowing of the leaves. Full sun is best, although it tolerates partial shade well. Space plants 24 to 40 inches apart. Hardy to zone 3.

Care: Easy. Some support probably will be necessary in windy areas. It has no serious pests. Division is rarely required for rejuvenation, which is fortunate, since division of old clumps is difficult because of the dense, deep roots. It is frequently unsuccessful, but if attempted, should be performed in late summer.

Tiarella cordifolia (Foamflower). Saxifrage family. Native from Nova Scotia to Georgia and Alabama.

The foamflower forms dense patches of clean, dark leaves topped with creamy, airy sprays of flowers in May and June. It is a woodland plant that is most useful as a ground cover and for naturalizing in areas of partial to deep shade.

The flowers are tiny and gathered in fluffy, delicate sprays above the foliage, creating a foamy effect, true to their name.

The dark green leaves are dense and lush all season. Growing to about 4 inches long, they are oval and toothed. The leaves are held perpendicular to short, erect stems, creating a flat, even, solid mass of foliage about 6 inches high. The flowering stems arise as much as 12 inches above the foliage.

The foamflower spreads by underground stolons, but could never be considered invasive. It is long-lived, and will form broad patches in time.

How to Start: Divisions should be planted in the spring. Seed is best sown outdoors when collected ripe in late summer. It can be sown in early spring if first prechilled in the refrigerator.

Where to Plant: Moist loam rich in organic matter is best. Give them partial to deep shade. Space plants 12 inches apart. Hardy to zone 3.

Care: Easy. While the plant thrives on abundant moisture, it requires little special attention. It has no serious pests. It occasionally requires division to check its spread. This is also an excellent means of increase, and the stolons are easy to dig and divide in the spring.

Tradescantia virginiana (Spiderwort). Spiderwort family. Native to the eastern United States.

Adaptable to many difficult situations, including infertile soil, deep shade, and boggy conditions, the spiderwort will provide colorful flowers over a long season. It can, however, have a tendency to sprawl and spread through the garden when it is not restrained. Named cultivars are usually superior to the native species.

Top: *Thermopsis caroliniana*
Above: *Tiarella* species

Tradescantia virginiana

The flowers are usually bright purple, although many cultivars have been selected that are white, blue, purple, pink, or red. The blossoms are composed of three petals, are about 1 inch wide, and last individually for only a day; however, they are produced in clusters at the ends of the stems and bloom over a long season, from June to September.

The deep green leaves are almost straplike, growing to 1 inch wide and as long as 15 inches. The lower portion of the leaf is wrapped around the stem, giving the plant the appearance of a coarse grass. The form is variable, but mostly upright, and the plant is from 18 to 36 inches high. The stems are angled at the joints. From midseason on, the plant will tend to sprawl into an open, tangled structure.

Spiderwort will spread enthusiastically by underground stems, and by aboveground stems that root where their joints contact the soil. It is long-lived, but requires frequent division to restrain its rampant growth.

How to Start: The species is easy to start by seed sown in the spring, but best results will occur from fresh seed collected and sown in late summer. Germination takes about 2 weeks. Nursery plants or divisions of named cultivars should be planted in spring.

Where to Plant: Spiderwort tolerates nearly any soil, but grows most vigorously in moist, rich ones, which should be avoided by gardeners who want to contain the growth. Give it full sun to deep shade. Space plants 15 to 30 inches apart. Native to moist soils in the eastern United States, it is hardy to zone 4.

Care: Easy, but it can be moderately difficult to restrain. The plant will look best with adequate water. If the stems flop badly in midsummer, they can be cut clear to the ground; the revived plant will flower again in the fall.

The plant has few serious pests, although several caterpillars have been reported. Botrytis blight may attack the blossoms.

Division is best performed every other year, and should be done every third or fourth year to control spreading. It is an excellent means of increase, and should be done in the spring.

Trollius europaeus (Common Globe Flower). Buttercup family. Native to Europe and arctic North America.

Globe flowers are leafy, bushy plants that produce rounded, globular blossoms in many shades of yellow and orange. Blooming in late spring and early summer, they are an excellent choice for moist, heavy soil unsuitable for most other perennials.

Flowers come in many shades of yellow and orange, according to variety. They are 1 to 3 inches across and are composed of five to fifteen showy sepals in a rounded, ball-like mass that looks as if it has never fully opened. The flowers appear on the ends of long stems in May and June.

The dark green leaves are deeply divided into three to five lobes and have a medium texture. The basal leaves have stalks, and are larger and denser than the stem leaves, whose bottom portions wrap around the stems. The stems grow 1 to 3 feet tall, depending upon cultivar, and in upright clusters, creating bushy, rounded masses. The foliage is attractive all season.

Globe flowers are long-lived and restrained in growth. The clumps gradually expand by sending up new shoots on the outside perimeter of the crown.

How to Start: Planting divisions in late summer is the best method. Plants can also be started from seed first frozen for 2 days in the refrigerator, then sown outdoors in late summer. Fresh seed germinates well in 6 or 7 weeks. Old seed may take 2 years or more to sprout.

Where to Plant: Fertile, very moist soil high in organic matter is best, but avoid boggy conditions. While preferring partial shade, globe flowers tolerate full sun if the soil is kept moist. Space plants 12 inches apart. Hardy to zone 3.

Care: Easy in moist soil. Remove faded flowers to prolong the flowering period. Keep well watered, as these plants must never dry out. They have no serious pests. The plant usually requires division every 5 years or so to reduce crowding, but if necessary can survive much longer without disturbance. An excellent means of increase, division should be done in late summer.

Veronica **species** (Speedwell). Snapdragon family. Of diverse often hybrid origin; generally native to Europe and Asia.

The colorful spikes of veronica make quite a show in July and August. Many cultivars are available, and most are selected from crosses between *Veronica longifolia* and *V. spicata*.

The flowers are usually blue, although varieties are available in pink, purple, and white. Individually they are small and gathered into dense, narrow spikes at the ends of the branches. They bloom in late June through the middle of August.

The light green leaves sometimes have a grayish cast, are lance-shaped, and about 2 inches long. Of medium texture, they grow opposite one another on the upright stems. The plant produces bushy clusters of stems that can be either branched or unbranched. Varieties range in size from 12 to 30 inches tall, although most grow to around 18 inches.

Most varieties are long-lived and fairly restrained in growth. The clumps enlarge by sending up many new shoots at the perimeter.

How to Start: Named cultivars should be started by divisions planted in spring or fall. You can sow seed outdoors in the spring, but considerable variation will result from hybrid seed.

Where to Plant: The soil should not be overly fertile, but it must be well drained. Full sun is best, but the plant tolerates partial shade. Space plants 12 to 18 inches apart. Hardy to zone 4.

Trollius 'Orange Princess'

Veronica longifolia 'Blue Peter'

Care: Moderately easy. Removing faded flowers will prolong the flower season. Downy mildew and leaf spot can be serious problems, especially in humid areas. If these diseases are likely, protect the plants with a fungicide. Division probably is necessary every 4 years for the best appearance of most varieties. It is an excellent means of increase, and should be done either in the spring or fall.

Related Species and Cultivars: *Veronica incana* (Woolly Speedwell) has white, furry leaves on 12- to 18-inch stems. The foliage contrasts well with the pale blue flower spikes in June and July. This plant must have excellent drainage to survive wet winters.

V. latifolia 'Crater Lake Blue', formerly called *V. teucrium*, has bright blue flowers over a long season, nearly all summer long. It grows to 18 inches with a tangled, much-branched habit of growth.

V. longifolia (Clump Speedwell) bears light blue flowers on 12-inch plants from July through August.

V. spicata (Spike Speedwell) is similar to the above, growing 18 inches tall with many branches. The flower spikes are usually shorter, but are very densely produced.

Yucca filamentosa (Spanish Bayonet; Adam's Needle). Agave family. Native from North Carolina south to Florida and Mississippi.

The yucca's stiff, rigid leaves, tipped with a sharp spine, are arranged in dense, grayish-green rosettes that reach 30 inches high. In midsummer the plant produces very tall flower stalks, from 3 to 12 feet high, bearing many flowers. The plant provides an exotic, arid-climate appearance.

The flowers are white, more usually ivory, bell-shaped, 1 to 2 inches long, and appear in large vertical clusters on the upper one-third to one-half of the stalks. They bloom from June to the middle of August.

The lance-shaped, gray-green leaves are up to 2½ feet long, evergreen, and remain attractive throughout the year. They are arranged in basal rosettes up to 30 inches high.

The yucca grows slowly, spreading by offsets around its base, and is long-lived. It is often treated as a shrub in the landscape.

How to Start: Easy from seed sown in early spring, but this method takes 3 years or more to obtain a flowering-size plant. The more usual methods are to plant offsets or nursery plants in the spring. Long tap roots form quickly with this plant; so transplanting is best done when young.

Where to Plant: Yuccas tolerate many soils, as long as they are well drained. They are best, however, in a light, sandy soil. Give them full sun. Space plants 24 to 48 inches apart. Hardy to zone 4.

Care: Very easy. The plant is highly drought resistant. It has no serious pests. Division is seldom required for rejuvenation, but is an excellent means of propagation. Offsets may be dug in spring without disturbing the parent plant.

Yucca filamentosa

The formal design of this perennial garden is softened by the use of grass pathways and vine-covered arches.

Index

Page numbers in italics
indicate illustrations.